Jim Clark

A photographic portrait

Jim Clark OBE was born on 4 March 1936 on a farm near Kilmany, in Fife, Scotland, and was a farmer all his life as well as a World Champion racing driver. His favoured sports were cricket, shooting (on the farm) and water-skiing, and he enjoyed motoring, photography (with a Fujica Half camera) and flying his own aircraft. He liked the music of Louis Armstrong, Ella Fitzgerald, Frank Sinatra and The Beatles. He was popular with the opposite sex, but did not marry. He died on the Hockenheimring, near Heidelburg, Germany, on 7 April 1968.

© Quentin Spurring (photo commentary)
and Peter Windsor (introduction), 2008

Additional caption material by Peter Windsor

First published in March 2008

A catalogue record for this book is available from the British Library

ISBN 978 1 84425 501 6

Library of Congress control no 2007943087

Published by Haynes Publishing,
Sparkford, Yeovil, Somerset BA22 7JJ, UK
Tel: 01963 442030 Fax: 01963 440001
Int. tel: +44 1963 442030 Int. fax: +44 1963 440001
E-mail: sales@haynes.co.uk
Website: www.haynes.co.uk

Haynes North America Inc.
861 Lawrence Drive, Newbury Park,
California 91320, USA

All pictures in this book are courtesy of LAT Photographic, with the exception of pages 20, 26 + 27 (Graham Gauld), page 21 (David Ross), page 107 (Russ Lake), page 179 (The Klemantaski Collection), pages 190 + 207 (Bob Tronolone) and page 206 (Ed Heuvink)

The publisher wishes to thank all at LAT for their collaboration on this book, and in particular Peter Higham, Kathy Ager, Tim Wright, Kevin Wood, Stephen Carpenter, Matt Smith and Emma Champion

Design and layout by Richard Parsons

Printed and bound in Great Britain by
J. H. Haynes & Co. Ltd

CONTENTS PAGE Jim Clark concentrating hard behind the wheel of the 3-litre, H16 BRM-engined Lotus 43, on his way to third place in the 1966 Oulton Park Gold Cup.

Jim Clark
A photographic portrait

Photographs by **LAT** • Photo commentary by **Quentin Spurring** • Reminiscences by **Peter Windsor**

CONTENTS

Jim Clark

BY PETER WINDSOR

Your first question was what he'd be like. Would he look as he did in all those garland shots, white teeth flashing, black hair sweated-down by the famous dark blue-and-white Bell helmet? Or would he be a million miles away – the pensive, nail-biting artist whose flux of thought was travelling to who knows where?

It was hot that day in Sydney in '65. Ninety-three in the shade, with Esso, BP and KLG flags fluttering in a westerly. Loudspeakers filled the middle distance. In the foreground unrobed Brabhams, disconnected Climax fours and the pungency of Castrol R. Girls with bare midriffs and tight, thigh-length slacks giggled by the Shell tent. Over here, Scuderia Veloce (very David McKay, very immaculate).

Over there, Team Lotus – except that when they were thousands of miles from home, borrowing a trailer from the Geoghegan brothers and towing it with a Zephyr, they were obliged to call themselves 'Team Lotus'. Next to it, though, the heart of it all – a green-and-yellow, glinting, Lotus 32B-Climax. 'Team Lotus' down the sides, just as it should be (in the smaller print of that period). Red upholstery covering the best seat in the world. And next to it: mechanic/driver/semi-manager, Ray Parsons, bare-chested, in soldier's pose – back straight, arms to the side, head focused alternately on the back of the car and then on the shorter, sun-tanned man alongside him...

On Jim Clark, of Chirnside, Berwickshire, Scotland. The 1963 World Champion. And 1962 and '64 champion, give or take a loose oil line or two.

He was shorter than you expected – but then you'd only ever seen him in foggy, black-and-white photos. He, too, wore no shirt. Fawn trousers, pleated at the front. Westover driving shoes. Black Wayfarers. More legs than

torso. Slicked, combed, black hair. Perfect muscle tone. Perfect build for a racing driver.

The best in the world, no discussion.

And so you watched and waited and tried to imagine. Tried to imagine this man – standing just a few feet away, now examining his black, Pioneer goggles, holding them up to the sun – indeed being the driver you'd read about and whose career you'd attempted to follow through the patchy newspaper coverage and the months-old race reportage.

Tried to imagine that this Mr Clark – right here, chatting to Parsons – was indeed the 'quiet, unassuming Scottish farmer who enjoys the Kelso ram sales as much as he does the thrill of driving his Lotus 25 to victory in the world's toughest motor races'. That roasting day in February, transfixed at Warwick Farm, none of that for me ran true. Maybe it was because I was in awe; maybe it was because I was a kid.

Something about Jim Clark, however, made me shiver. Shy? Unassuming? These were the Clark adjectives of the moment. His aura, though, said something completely different: it said 'diamond-hard commitment'. It said: 'don't even think about it'. It said: 'push me if you dare'.

And so I called him 'Mr Clark'. I said 'please' and 'thank you' as I proffered my copy of *Jim Clark at the Wheel* and my red Biro. And then I left, book in hand.

February, 1966: a second World Championship and the Indy win now behind him, Jim Clark flies in to Mascot Airport, Sydney, with Trans-Australia Airlines. I walk on to the tarmac and go right up to him and offer to carry his bags. He says 'thank you very much', but that's the extent of our conversation. He has just flown

OPPOSITE Nürburgring 1961: First-time-out in a Formula 1 car on the 'Ring, Jim recovered from a major accident during qualifying to finish fourth in the Grand Prix of Europe.

Aintree 1962: The British Grand Prix crowd saw the first 'perfect' performance by Jim when he started on pole position, drove the fastest race lap and led from start to finish.

Peter Windsor to Jim Clark, Sydney airport, March 1968: "Jim, I'd love to have a life in motor racing. How can I do that? Would it be possible?"
Jim Clark to Peter Windsor: "Anything's possible. Just give it everything you've got. If you really want to work in motor sport you will do it. Never give up."

in from New Zealand and is wearing a red-and-white checked, short-sleeved shirt. Once I have loaded his Leston bag, he drives away in a car that will always live in the memory: a pinky-grey Toyota Corolla (with torsion bar suspension).

January, 1967: in the VIP lounge at Mascot, fresh – or looking fresh – from the flight from Johannesburg to Sydney, Mr Clark and Jackie Stewart sit in small-lapel suits, ties and white shirts, looking like guys out of a photoshoot for *Life*. The talk is of Pedro Rodriguez's amazing win in the opening round of the championship. Jackie leads, Jim chimes in when asked. He is polite, civil – but again the image is clear: you don't mess with Jim Clark. It's as if he doesn't need to say much in order to impose his presence. And thus the misconception – the one about him being 'quiet and retiring out of the car but changing completely when the goggles are up'. He didn't change (you thought at the time): he just kept his powder dry, as Bernie Ecclestone is fond of saying.

March, 1968: he walks into the Sydney terminal wearing a Munsing polo shirt, grey slacks and carrying a leather briefcase. He sees me there and asks me to have a coffee or a Coke while they try to fix the big Boeing 707's technical fault.

'Thank you, Mr Clark.'

'Jim, please.'

'Where are you flying to now?'

'To Los Angeles and then on to Indianapolis. We're testing there next week with the new turbine car.'

'Gosh. Good luck. One question I've always wanted to ask: why did you wear a dark blue peak instead of a white peak on your helmet at Zandvoort in 1964 and Mexico in 1966?'

'Blimey. Trying to remember. I think the white one must have broken or something like that and I had to borrow one – I think from Dan Gurney. At Zandvoort the problem was that I wore my goggles very tight to stop the sand creeping through the edges. They did that, but they also gave me a splitting headache!'

'But you had a perfect win that day! You walked away with it!'

'Well, not quite perfect: I hit a kerb at one point because I was thinking about the headache rather than the road ahead!'

'Oh, I see,' I said, before changing the subject to the previous weekend's race in Tasmania. Jim had been on the pole in the Gold Leaf 49 but had struggled, obviously, in the wet. 'What happened at Longford?' I asked. 'Why did Piers Courage win there?'

'Piers was very good. He had the skinny Dunlops and of course the F2 car was perfect for the conditions. I'm very pleased for Piers.'

Then the Big Question, fool that I was: 'Jim, I'd love to have a life in motor racing. How can I do that? Would it be possible?'

'Anything's possible. Just give it everything you've got. If you really, really want to work in motor sport you will do it. Never give up...'

He was gone, then, gathering up his things and returning to the departure gate. I was the last person in Australia ever to speak to him.

I guess the two biggest questions I have ever had about Jim Clark are these. First, how was someone so intelligent, so great at what he did, so noble (in the truest sense of the word) – how was this genius able to tolerate and wipe from his mind the catastrophic string of accidents and deaths with which he was confronted throughout his career? And, second, how was he able to do what he did in 1967 (and thus through into 1968) despite the following string of difficulties:

1) Due to Harold Wilson's insidious new (97 per cent!) income tax laws, Jim in mid-1966 was advised by his (local, Scots) advisers to set up residency in Pembroke, Bermuda and to base himself in Paris, France. As a result, he would not visit the UK for more than four or five days in 1967 (for the British GP plus a couple of other events); he would have to move all his personal possessions from his Edington Mains farmhouse; and (obviously) he would miss races he had always known and loved – the early-season F2 events, the Race of Champions, etc, etc. His 'home' was a shared flat in Paris; he was isolated from his non-racing friends and his family;

2) He broke up from his long-term girlfriend, Sally Stokes, in mid-1966. In early 1967 she announced her engagement to the Dutch sports car driver, Ed Swart;

3) Indy, already a mental and physical drain, wasn't even a race he could win in 1967. Let down by the late delivery of the BRM Indy engines, Lotus reverted at the last minute to the old 1965/66 cars. In between Indy tests, qualifying and the race, Jim raced in Europe and thus spent much of his time flying – economy class – in 707s and Caravelles;

4) For the first time in his life he had a genuine number one driver (Graham Hill) alongside him in the Lotus team. There was no doubt that Jim could beat Hill on equal terms – but how equal would they be in Lotus's first year with the Lotus 49-DFV, particularly when Graham additionally enjoyed a personal contract with Ford? This was precisely the situation that Michael Schumacher would never have tolerated – and which drove Fernando Alonso away from McLaren;

5) Lotus fragility hadn't improved. Jim suffered numerous suspension problems on the 49 (including a broken front suspension rocker at the Nürburgring and that famous rear suspension collapse at Watkins Glen) and on the F2 48 (from which a wheel came adrift at the Nürburgring's south circuit).

And yet despite all this – despite there being enough going on in one year to drive most athletes to retirement – Jim Clark in 1967 drove at least ten races that could have been nominated as his greatest. He'd miss connecting flights out of Indy, he'd lose his luggage, he'd drive his yellow Elan S3 coupé through the night, he'd get to Zolder, he'd borrow a helmet and some goggles from Eric Offenstadt or someone... and he'd be the fastest driver on the planet, despite the 48 being unkind to its tyres and in no way as easy to drive as a Brabham. How did he do it? What was he thinking as he sat snug in the Elan, it's 1600cc twin-cam hauling him along?

He was thinking of the details, certainly. He was a detail man. He constantly thought through his racing problems – and the more he talked to Colin Chapman about them, the more the solutions were obvious. He, not Chapman, came up with the idea of tacking a small rear wing on to the back of the 49 in New Zealand, where, in Chapman's absence, he was part-mechanic, part-manager and full-time driver. He would personally adjust tyre pressures. He would supervise the repainting of the 49 in Gold Leaf colours. He would represent Gold Leaf interests against the political forces of CAMS (the Confederation of Australian Motor Sport).

Nor can we dismiss the question with platitudes about Jim being 'indecisive' or 'introvert'. We owe him more than that. Ford's Walter Hayes liked to tell the story of how he felt obliged early in 1967 to 'phone Jim and point out that Ford were paying Graham much more than he, Jim, was currently receiving and how he had to plead, virtually, for Jim to accept a rise. I don't buy that. I buy the 'phone call – but I don't buy Jim's supposed naïvety. Jim always knew what he was doing and he was very aware of his earning power; the point was that he had to do things his way, on his terms. He knew that Hayes would ring him; he waited for Hayes to ring him. Call it 'stubborn'.

Call it one of the reasons why he was so good for so long.

Consider, too, why Jim decided on Bermuda/Paris in 1967 (and beyond) when he could have chosen the obvious home of Switzerland, like Jackie Stewart and many others who would follow him. Why Paris? Why Bermuda? Friends like Jo Bonnier and Sir John Whitmore would have pointed to Switzerland or Monaco. They were the obvious places; they were the havens, early though this was in the age of the 'celebrity tax exile'.

Jim took a completely different route. I think he did this because he wouldn't take the standard path any more than he would give his closest friend – Jackie Stewart – any meaningful information about braking points, gear ratios or tyre pressures. He was Jim Clark. And he wasn't unassuming or compliant – in or out of the car. What made him a gentleman and perhaps the greatest driver we've ever seen was that he didn't have to talk about it. His driving did the talking.

And so he took the advice of two Scots from the Borders, from his home town, and from a friend of a friend who knew about this Commonwealth country called Bermuda.

To me, this was much like the time at Snetterton,

He constantly thought through his racing problems – and the more he talked to Colin Chapman about them, the more the solutions were obvious. He, not Chapman, came up with the idea of tacking a small rear wing on to the back of the 49 in New Zealand, where, in Chapman's absence, he was part-mechanic, part-manager and full-time driver.

Andrew Ferguson on Jim: "Well, he'd sit around the office at Cheshunt and we'd argue about who paid which half of the dinner bill at the previous race and then finally he'd get up and leave and he'd turn around and say, 'You know, you'll miss be when I'm gone'. He often said that, and – you know what? – he was right. We missed him all right."

I think in 1964, when Jim was at the circuit only to present a trophy. During the course of the day he was casually invited for a drink at a hospitality tent, but when he decided to take up the offer he was asked by a guard at the gate for his appropriate credential. When Jim replied that he had none, but that he had been invited nonetheless, the guard – who was only doing his job – said that he would have to go and speak to his superior. He did so, and received a go-ahead... but Jim was gone by the time he returned to the door. His rationale? If they couldn't be bothered to leave his name at the door, having invited him, then he'd be blowed if he'd hang around and invite himself in. Slightly precious? On the contrary, I think this was a reminder that Clark's 'quiet, shy demeanour' in reality encased a character that was as granite-hard as Michael Schumacher's.

I suspect, too, that Jim's relatively unobtrusive demeanour was also a function of his genius. Consider that he was an artist of a driver who at the very least is right up there with the best of them in history, shoulder-to-shoulder with Juan Manuel Fangio, Stirling Moss, Jackie Stewart, Ayrton Senna and Michael Schumacher – and who may have been better than all of these – and you have to consider also the side effects of that brilliance.

In Moss's case it was a penchant for racing only British cars; Michael showed an occasional disregard for the sporting ethic; Ayrton wasn't Fangio when it came to racing for the right team at the right time.

And Jim Clark – out of the car – was this very private, indecisive Scot. It wasn't that he was just protective of his privacy; he hated public acclaim. It embarrassed him.

I once asked Sally Stokes, Jim's girlfriend from 1963 to '66, how he felt after a win – how he felt when he had left the circuit and they were on their way to the airport or hotel or whatever. She replied that he would say something like 'well, that was good', and would then immediately change the subject to where they were going to eat, or what film they were going to see.

In all of this, we shouldn't under-estimate, of course, the effect of Colin Chapman and Lotus on the character of Jim Clark. Unlike Fangio, who picked and chose the teams for which he would race, year on year, and unlike Stirling, who was urbane and self-sufficient virtually from the day he could walk, or Jackie, who loved the business side of F1 as much as he loved driving the cars, Jim grew up in a solid, conservative, disciplined Scots family before working all his life for Colin Chapman. Colin was suave and clever; Colin built the most gorgeous of racing cars; Colin was a winner – but Colin was also a man who expected his staff to work basically only for food and to take holidays about once a decade.

Long after he won his first World Championship, Jim was slated to share hotel rooms in order to hold down the costs. His expenses were dissected with a scalpel. When I asked Andrew Ferguson, Lotus's Team Manager, what he most remembered about Jim, he replied, 'Well, he'd sit around the office at Cheshunt and we'd argue about who paid which half of the dinner bill at the previous race, and then finally he'd get up and leave and he'd turn around and say, "You know, you'll miss me when I'm gone". He often said that, and – you know what? – he was right. We missed him all right.'

You could see this in the small print that would accompany Lotus's delivery of a new Elan to Jim. Forgetting the publicity and endorsement Jim would give them, it would be made clear in a covering letter that precisely £1,832 12s 6d (or whatever) would be deducted from Jim's next retainer and that an additional amount would be held in reserve to cover any damage, etc. All OK if you're dealing with a mechanic or someone. Jim Clark? In the Lotus hierarchy, he was only a step or two above the mechanics.

On February 14, 1968, therefore, it's no surprise to find Jim sitting down at the desk in his room at the Rushcutter's Bay Travelodge in Sydney and writing a letter to his flatmate, Jabby Crombac, in Paris. He talks about the Tasman Series to date, and the problems Team Lotus are facing with CAMS regarding the cigarette advertising, but the thrust of the letter is about something else.

'One other thing occurs to me,' he says. 'The log book for the Elan and insurance certificate are in the glovebox, both [triple underlined!] of which should be returned to Andrew [Ferguson] so that he can get the licence renewed. I don't know if Colin has made any final decisions with regard to swapping the Elans around, but I will be writing to him soon, and will remind him...'

All was detailed and organised – but why were Lotus leaving Jim Clark to worry about such trivia? The answer is that this was the way Lotus always did it – and Jim, I guess, didn't know life any differently. He'd dine with Jackie and Helen Stewart and at the end of the meal there would be the usual routine with the bill: who ate what and at what price?

He did change, though, in 1967. It was impossible for him not to change. He was single and he was based in Paris. He was earning increasingly more. He was part of society's elite. He stood up more to Colin Chapman, to what he saw as unnecessary risks – such as the gauge of the metal on the 49's suspension arms. He tempered his driving a little, aware that the 49 was not yet rock-solid and that he would perhaps be out-shone from time to time in qualifying by his team-mate, Graham Hill, but he didn't rise to the pressure. He stayed quiet – as quiet as he always was. He grew his hair a little longer; he worked hard on not biting his nails. He didn't over-dress, he didn't under-dress. He spent most of his life in the cockpit of Lotus racing cars, in planes – and in his road cars (his Elan and his Ford Galaxie). In '67, as in previous years, Jim drove about 40,000 miles on the road. He loved the privacy of the cars.

And then, out of the blue, he invited Jackie and Helen and Jochen and Nina Rindt to his Bermuda apartment after the 1967 US Grand Prix. The place wasn't particularly lavish; there was no furniture of which to speak. This, though, was a little bit of the Tasman Series re-captured. Jim needed it after a long and ultimately disappointing year.

It didn't last. Mexico loomed – and then came the telegram from Western Union: 'Everything is all set for Ford in Rockingham race of October 29. Please call collect to confirm. Best Regards, John Holman (Holman & Moody).'

Jim had been fascinated by NASCAR stockers when he first saw them in 1964 at Daytona, where he was racing a Ford Cortina Lotus as part of the Speed Week. He'd quickly embraced not only Indianapolis but also the full palette of US motor racing. He liked the variety and he especially respected the money. Now he was to race in a NASCAR event for the first time.

Jim didn't drive just anything. He once refused to race a Lotus 19 at Mosport because he didn't like its preparation; and he resisted an offer from AJ Foyt to jump into a sprint car at Springfield in 1963. Generally, though, we obtain further insight into Clark when we appreciate just how much he loved to drive what he would describe as 'interesting' cars in 'interesting' locations.

In addition to his regular commitments, first for Border Reivers and then for Team Lotus, there were numerous examples of 'interesting' cars in 'interesting' locations: a few 'fun' laps in an ERA at Rouen, a Ferrari 330P4 on a private track in France and the fearsome Lycoming Special in New Zealand; a Lotus 21 F1 car and the Lotus 38 Indy car up the hills at Ollon-Villars and Les Rangiers; the four-wheel-drive Felday at Brands Hatch in 1966; the Cortina-Lotus in the '66 RAC Rally; the Parnelli Jones Paxton turbine car at Indy in '67; Minis, Lotus Elans, Ford Galaxies and of course many Cortina-Lotus cars in various saloon car events; the Rockingham NASCAR Ford; one-off drives in privately entered Lotus 19s and 23s in both the States and the UK...

Study of Jim's schedule in the month before the 1967 Italian Grand Prix – a race that many consider to have been among his greatest – provides a further view of the speed of his life:

- Sunday, August 6: drive back to Paris from the German GP at the Nürburgring (Lotus Elan).
- Thursday, August 10: fly (privately) to Karlskoga, Sweden.
- Sunday, August 13: F2 Swedish GP; fly to Paris in the evening.
- Thursday, August 17: fly (privately) to Enna, Sicily.
- Sunday, August 20: F2 Mediterranean GP; fly to Paris in the evening.
- Wednesday, August 23: fly to Toronto for the Canadian GP.
- Sunday, August 27: Canadian GP; fly to Paris in the evening.
- Thursday, August 31: fly (privately) to Helsinki.
- Sunday, September 3 : F2 Suomen GP.
- Monday, September 4: drive to Hameenlinna.
- Tuesday, September 5: F2 Hameenlinna GP; fly to Paris in the evening.
- Wednesday, September 6: fly to Milan, Italian GP.
- Sunday, September 10: Italian GP; fly to Paris in the evening.

He stood up to Colin Chapman – to what he saw as unnecessary risks... He tempered his driving a little, aware that the 49 was not yet rock-solid and that he would perhaps be out-shone from time to time in qualifying by his team-mate Graham Hill, but he didn't rise to the pressure. He stayed quiet – as quiet as he always was.

OPPOSITE Monza 1965: From the pole, Jim was in a classic, slipstreaming battle until an electrical failure intervened late in the Italian Grand Prix. A new lap record was scant consolation.

No-one compensated better. No-one maximised a difficult car the way Jim Clark maximised them. No-one better massaged the tyres. No-one was more sensitive to the slightest glitches in car performance and no-one was more capable of working with the problems.

That's quite a lot of flying, quite a lot of suitcase-packing, quite a lot of open-road driving and quite a lot of laundry, leaving little time for an athlete to drive at his peak in what was perhaps the most dangerous era in the history of motor sport. And to put his Monza drive into its full context, consider too that Jim's next race was with the F2 Lotus 48 in Albi, France. The greatest driver in the world – the man who had just unlapped himself at Monza – 12 days later spun his tyre-thirsty, twitchy 48 on the quick left-hander behind the pits and narrowly missed a concrete bridge abutment. In front of maybe 5,000 spectators. With but a couple of mechanics awaiting him in the pits.

Ergo: Jim's commitment to F2 and to other, lesser events was no less than that of F1. He was a total professional, empty track or full, difficult F2 car or sublime 33B. And Hockenheim 1968, could have been Rouen '67 (where he lost it before the Nouveau Monde hairpin due to a puncture) or, indeed, Albi '67. No wonder Jim developed that 'armour' of privacy; for what, in a detailed, complete racing sense, was there to talk about?

I say 'sublime' Lotus 33B: it was easy for Jim's opponents, and for the press, and therefore the public, to assume that Jim enjoyed a huge car advantage for much of his career. Jim drove enough great races in bad cars, however, for the reverse to be true. No-one compensated better. No-one maximised a difficult car the way Jim Clark maximised them. No-one better massaged the tyres. No-one was more sensitive to the slightest glitches in car performance and no-one was more capable of working with the problems. Jochen Rindt and Jackie Stewart knew that from their F2 races against Jim. The public saw that for themselves in 1966, when Jim regularly upstaged the 3-litre F1 cars with the 2-litre Lotus 33B-Climax – and then later in the year became the only driver ever to win with the horrendously unwieldy 3-litre BRM H16 engine.

And of course it wasn't easy – even in the 25 and the 33 – because a good car is only the half of it. A great car is a function of a great driver because perfect 'manipulative' drivers – by which I mean drivers who manage, or manipulate the dynamic energy of the car, as distinct from spending their time on the edge, reacting to the energy of the car – know instinctively what they can give to, and take from, a car in order to reduce the lap time. There's no element of making the car 'easy to drive'; a great driver isn't an articulate, detailed 'test' driver. He just knows. He tells his guys what he needs. And then he does it.

As Jim Clark did in the 1963 French GP – a race that appears on paper to have been yet another walkover win with the ground-breaking, monocoque 25. As it happened, Jim was far from confident as practice began:

'The long straights of Reims were a problem,' he wrote afterwards, 'for the Lotus was certainly not the fastest Grand Prix car, even though a correspondent in *Autosport* claimed at the end of the season that it was. Things didn't look good, so in practice I began to experiment and form my race plan...'

As we now know, Jim drove probably the best opening two race laps of his career at Reims, perfectly managing the 25 through the fast corners and opening a psychologically damaging gap on the field; he gradually pulled away, only for his Climax V8 to slow with two broken valve springs. Nursing the fluffy engine and wearing Dunlops, Jim was 'saved' by the rain: it came down to perfect manipulation of the car in low-grip, unpredictable conditions. Jim Clark finished the French GP in a class of his own.

I like his reference to 'experimentation'. Like Lewis Hamilton today, Jim was unafraid to play around with the car when it didn't matter – on 'untimed' Fridays, or private tests, or even non-championship races. At Warwick Farm in '68 he spent a couple of laps on the Friday waving bystanders away from the outside of The Causeway – a double-apex left-hander behind the pits. And then, grass clear, he lost it with grace, spinning 360 degrees on the grass before rejoining the circuit.

The consequences had been much more severe at Aintree in '64, when he hit the straw bales hard while dicing with Graham Hill and lapping André Pilette, and then at Brands in '65, when he thumped an earth bank behind the pits after running wide out of Bottom Bend in the Race of Champions. At the time, he was right behind his close friend Dan Gurney. What had happened? How could Jim Clark have made such an error?

'First, the race was not terribly important,' he responded. 'Second, I knew Dan was on the latest Goodyears. I wanted to push him as hard as I could so that we could see where we stood with the Dunlops.

The track was damp and I knew that I could let Dan past and still retake the lead. What I wanted to do was push on hard and test Dan's Goodyears to the limit…'

Jim had none of Jackie Stewart's passion when it came to making racing safer. He had been racing longer and had seen all those accidents – had been there or had known Archie Scott-Brown, Harry Schell, Shane Summers, Chris Bristow, Alan Stacey, Taffy von Trips, Ricardo Rodriguez, Gary Hocking, Doug Revson, Timmy Mayer, Lex Davison, Rocky Tresise, Ian Raby, John Taylor, Bob Anderson, Lorenzo Bandini and several more. It was almost as if he had become immune to the problem. He raced with seat belts at Indy, in some sports cars and in the Cortina-Lotus, and yet he raced without them in a Lotus 49 at the Nürburgring. He usually upgraded every year with the latest helmets and overalls but he never thought of matching seat belts with a higher rollover bar. He raced past exposed trees without even thinking about it.

And yet he *did* care about safety; of course he did. His fingernails were bitten to the quick because he knew that he would always be able to take a racing car into territory from which all his peers would shy away; and he knew that venturing into that territory would be exponentially dangerous. The detail of accidents and accident-prevention? I think these were some of the subjects that Jim kept hidden from others and from his own consciousness. For what was the point? Accidents happened. They couldn't be prevented. And they were best filed away. Once, when Colin left the road in a rented Peugeot *en route* to the '65 French GP, and Sally had been tossed into the windscreen, he had fainted at the sight of Sally's blood.

Thus there were the other things with which he concerned himself. The next race. Possibly buying the Beagle aircraft company. Flying. Travelling to the next race. The cars. Day-to-day living in Paris. The farm in Scotland. The family. The tax man. Plans for a new Jim Clark driving jacket. For the most part, his life passed in a blur of circuits, planes, cars and hotel rooms.

And he was good. No, not good. Brilliant. The best. He was instinctively a perfect, manipulative driver. For Clark, hitting one kerb in one full-length Grand Prix was a Major Error. Jackie Stewart saw him in 1960, racing a Formula Junior Lotus 18 at Oulton Park. 'Right then it was obvious,' he says. 'The smoothness, the relaxed poise, the angle of the head in the cockpit.'

Thus Jim Clark loved the business of taking a new Chapman design, testing it, developing it, talking about it over dinner, talking about it at the factory – and then winning with it. It wasn't Jim Clark and Team Lotus; Jim Clark was Team Lotus – an inextricable, irreplaceable part of the whole.

Asked once about when he might retire, Jim replied, 'I don't know – but I do know this: I will retire to the farm and I will retire quite young.' He left the door open every year with 12-month contracts. And yet he didn't retire. He didn't retire after struggling with the 2-litre car in '66. He didn't retire after all the upheavals of '67. He loved the thought of racing the wedge-shaped 56 at Indy; he wanted to win the championship with the 49; and Colin had adopted Jim's innovative left-foot-braking idea for the new de Dion F2 Lotus 57.

People love to say that Jim would have hated the modern sponsorship era, would have hated the money and the politics – but look at him: he embraced the STP Lotus at Indy with its whitewall tyres; he was proud of the Gold Leaf livery on the other cars. And he respected money and those who wanted to pay him well for doing what he did to perfection. He loved those things, I think, because he loved the cars and solving the problems they posed. If sponsorship was a part of it then so, Andy Granatelli, be it. He was a brilliant driver and athlete who travelled in a suit and tie. He was a David Bailey counterpoint for Jean Shrimpton. He was a Borders farmer, a brother and a son in a closely knit, dignified family.

Last word, then, to the terribly civil but nonetheless heartfelt words of Colin Chapman, written at a time when Colin was a David Niven lookalike:

'If Jimmy was to retire tomorrow,' he said in 1965, 'I would like to remember him as someone who created a name and a personality of the highest possible calibre. There are other racing drivers who have generally to attract attention to themselves to make up for a lack of ability; but Jimmy has not had to do any of that and if he left racing tomorrow he would leave motor racing with an example which others would find hard to follow.'

With the benefit of the years since Hockenheim, 1968, an amendment to those words is now due:

Make Jim Clark 'impossible to follow'.

Colin Chapman, 1965: "There are other racing drivers who have generally to attract attention to themselves to make up for a lack of ability; but Jimmy has not had to do any of that and if he left racing tomorrow he would leave motor racing with an example which others would find hard to follow."

LEARNING TO WIN WITH THE REIVERS

BELOW James Clark Sr handed down his Sunbeam Talbot without realising that it would start his son on a road to motor racing stardom He later replaced it with a Mk3 version and sprinted, raced and rallied both cars extensively. This is an autotest at Leith Fort in Edinburgh.
(Photo courtesy of Graham Gauld)

James Clark, a well-to-do Scottish farmer, relocated his family south from Kilmany, Fife, to Chirnside, Berwickshire, when its youngest member was six years old. Young Jim was sent away to the famous Loretto boarding school in Edinburgh, but was taken out of school at the age of 16 because his father wanted him to work on the family's farms. A pastoral future seemed assured.

A year later, the future changed. Jim passed his driving test and, as the proud new keeper of his father's discarded Sunbeam Talbot, unknowingly embarked on his adventure with motor racing as a newly signed up member of his local Berwick & District Motor Club. Encouraged by a Chirnside garage owner, Jock McBain, he drove the Sunbeam in local rallies, autotests and an autocross during the summers of 1954 and 1955.

He competed on the 1955 International Scottish Rally, co-driving an Austin-Healey 100 for Billy Potts, a neighbouring farmer.

Potts was Jim's cousin, but his immediate family disapproved of the sport he had chosen. We owe the emergence of one of the greatest racing drivers the world has ever seen to his friendship with Ian Scott-Watson, the son of another neighbouring farmer. The two spectated together at race meetings at Charterhall, their local circuit, and Scott-Watson became a dedicated motorsport enthusiast, competing in all types of amateur events with his DKW saloon. Jim sometimes navigated for him on rallies.

Jim entered his first track event, a minor club sprint, on 3 June 1956 – the day Pete Collins, in a Ferrari, won the Belgian Grand Prix at Spa-Francorchamps. For the speed début of 19-year-old Jimmy, the scene was less glamorous: concrete army roadways on the bleak Stobs Military Camp, an old training facility near Hawick, about 30 miles from home. He was a winner first-time-out – the Sunbeam was the only finisher in its class. He competed in his first race a fortnight later.

Convinced that his young friend was a 'natural', Scott-Watson set out to prove it behind the backs of Clark's parents and his four older sisters – and without telling Jim, either. He entered his 'Deek' for a saloon handicap and a sportscar race on the Crimond aerodrome circuit near Peterhead, in the far north-east of Scotland, and Jim went along to help. Once there, Scott-Watson startled Clark by telling him that he was to drive in the sportscar race. Jim reckoned they might be far enough from home to hope that his family never found out, and decided to have a go. He wrote in his autobiography: "I felt I was on

On the programme:

ABERDEEN & DISTRICT MOTOR CLUB LTD.

CRIMOND RACE MEETING

SATURDAY, 16th JUNE, 1956

Held under the International Sporting Code of the F.I.A. and the General Competition Rules of the R.A.C. and S.A.C.U.

S.A.C.U. Open Permit No. A 278.   R.A.C. Restricted Permit No. D/1911.

"MOTOR RACING IS DANGEROUS
AND PERSONS ATTENDING THIS MEETING DO SO ENTIRELY AT THEIR OWN RISK"

It is a condition of admission that all persons having any connection with the promotion and/or organisation and/or conduct of the meeting, including the owners of the land and the drivers and owners of the vehicles, are absolved from all liability arising out of accidents howsoever caused resulting in damage and/or personal injury to spectators.

OFFICIAL 1/- PROGRAMME

---

hallowed ground. To me, racing was something that was almost sacred and not for me to touch."

The little 'Deek' was hopelessly outclassed and finished a solid last. But Jim lapped it three seconds faster than its owner, who was consequently accused of sandbagging during practice, and rehandicapped out of contention for the saloon race...

The first time, perhaps, that Jimmy got a real taste for this sport came that September in another club sprint, at Winfield, an airfield course a few miles from home. He was the winner of four classes, driving both the Sunbeam and the quaint DKW.

In 1957, Scott-Watson acquired a more effective car, a Porsche 356. Having contested another couple of races at Charterhall with the DKW and the Sunbeam, Jim raced the Porsche there in the first meeting run by the new Border Motor Racing Club. On a wet track, he surprised everyone, including himself, by beating several faster Austin-Healeys to win the trophy race. It was becoming clear that this farmer's son had been blessed with an extraordinary talent for driving cars. Over the following winter, Scott-Watson conspired with Jock McBain to give him a pukka racing car.

McBain was the driving force behind a loose-knit Scottish motorsport team, the Border Reivers. It was named for the 'raiders' or 'plunderers' who, in tribal groups, dominated the lawless region between the

established kingdoms of England and Scotland until the 17th century. They robbed, blackmailed, kidnapped and sometimes murdered each other for more than 300 years. For Sassenachs, their romantic legacy is a little difficult to grasp...

For the 1958 season, the team bought a competition thoroughbred, a second-hand Jaguar D Type, and McBain told Jim that he wanted him to race it. Jim thought he was mad, even after testing the car at Charterhall. But he was persuaded. In April, he drove the D Type on icy roads to York for the first meeting on the Full Sutton USAF base, where he then won two races. The opposition was weak, but he became the first man ever to average more than 100mph in a sports car on a British circuit. Three weeks later, Jim drove the Jaguar for a second time at Charterhall, where he had his first racing accident, sliding harmlessly through a fence due to a brake failure.

Three weeks after that, the Border Reivers raided Belgium – bringing Jimmy a brutal introduction to the big time. Jim's entire experience was limited to a dozen club races, but he was entered for the big Spa Grand Prix sportscar race, against top-level opposition. Jim was genuinely frightened by the fast and dangerous Francorchamps road course, and the race was run in typical Ardennes weather. One shower caught out the leader, Archie Scott-Brown. The works Lister crashed into a field and caught fire, and the popular little Scottish

ABOVE Jim Clark's very first race start, at Crimond in June 1956. J.L. Fraser's Lotus 11 in the foreground completed a 1–2–3 for Lotus 11 sports-racing cars behind Brian Naylor, who won 27 club races that season with his Maserati-engined car, and Borders farmer Jimmy Somervail in the Border Reivers entry. Also pictured are Kenny McLennan's Kieft-MG, John Campbell's MGA and, at left, A.R. Millar's Saltire. Clark finished very, very last with the ungainly 'Deek'.
(Photo and programme courtesy of David Ross)

ABOVE Jim's first race was in this 900cc, three-cylinder, two-stroke, front-drive DKW Sonderklasse – the forerunner of the Auto Union 1000, and a popular car in amateur European motorsport circles at the time. This is its owner, Ian Scott-Watson, competing in 1957.

driver succumbed to his burns in hospital. This accident, and the frights he had had, affected Jim deeply and forever tainted his relationship with the Spa circuit. He hated the place.

He thought of giving up this dangerous sport of track racing, and simply to continue in amateur rallies and speed events with his latest road car, a Triumph TR3. But Jim began to master the 3.4-litre D Type, and became increasingly successful. At Charterhall in September, his Jaguar was beaten by Innes Ireland (Tojeiro-Jaguar) and Ron Flockhart in the Le Mans winning 3.8-litre D Type, both entered by Ecurie Ecosse. McBain and his Border Reivers friends enjoyed a fierce rivalry with David Murray's more accomplished team and, despite the defeat, this event convinced Jim that he could be competitive at a higher level. He said of it: "I think this was the first time I drove the D Type to its limit. It gave me a great deal of confidence, because I realised that I could at least keep up with people of that stature."

The following month, Jim's Triumph won the Border Rally, a round of the Scottish championship – and then he abruptly found himself in the cockpit of a single-seater at Brands Hatch. McBain and Scott-Watson had decided that the Border Reivers should enter Formula 2, and had

arranged for Jim to join Graham Hill, Innes Ireland, Alan Stacey and others on a Lotus test day. Colin Chapman had not been told that Clark had never driven a single-seater, nor even seen Brands Hatch since once spectating there as a schoolboy. He was surprised when Jim lapped within 1.5sec of Hill. Later, a wheel fell off the Lotus 12 as Hill was in mid-corner at Paddock Hill Bend, and the car rolled, throwing out its driver. Jim was shocked: "I said I wouldn't drive that car. I wasn't going to have anything to do with something that broke like that..."

On the same day, however, Jim drove the prototype Lotus Elite, and loved it. A deal was done for Scott-Watson to buy a pre-production Elite, and the car was ready just in time for the Boxing Day meeting at Brands Hatch. Jim outpaced all the opposition, including Chapman himself in another Elite. That was the day the boss of Team Lotus realised that this modest young farmer was special.

For the 1959 season, Border Reivers, mindful of Jim's apparent aversion to single-seaters, replaced the D Type with a second-hand Lister-Jaguar. Despite family rows at home, Jim was now keen to commit his weekends to racing and gained confidence steadily. Out of the cars, he remained rather a tense personality, given to chewing his nails, outwardly lacking in self-assurance. This was his busiest season yet (although interrupted for five weeks in late summer, while he attended to the harvest back on the farm). As it progressed, increasingly the diffidence disappeared when he was in the cockpits of racing cars.

In mid-season, there were two more continental forays. Border Reivers entered its Elite for the Le Mans 24 Hours and sent it to Lotus for its pre-race preparation, but Chapman's company failed to finish the work on time. Chapman offered a works Elite, which Jim co-drove with John Whitmore. Scott-Watson bought this car and Jim's next race with it was the first event in the 'Autosport' World Cup (a four-race Anglo-Dutch team contest) at Zandvoort, where its rear axle seized when it was leading. Thereafter, however, it became a regular winner in his hands, and Jim scored a win and a second place in the second and final World Cup meeting at Brands Hatch. It was also at Brands Hatch, back for the Boxing Day meeting, that Jim raced a first single-seater for the first time.

Jim and Border Reivers had had a great season, winning 13 races from 24 starts with the Lister, and seven from 14 with the two Elites. Thirty podiums from a grand total of 41 starts made Jim the most talked about young amateur driver in Britain. He was approached by Reg Parnell, the manager of the Aston Martin team that had just won Le Mans and the World Sports Car Championship. McBain, who was friendly with Parnell, had urged him to test his unusually talented Border Reivers driver for the new Aston Martin Formula 1 team. Jim had two trials in a DBR4 prototype at Goodwood early in 1960, but was also being courted by Colin Chapman. A Team Lotus transporter 'coincidentally' rolled into Goodwood on the day of the second test, and Mike Costin asked Parnell if he could ask Jim to try the Formula Junior Lotus 18. Jim was impressed by the power of the Aston Martin – but astonished by the "fantastic" roadholding of the Lotus, which he lapped 4sec under the Formula 3 lap record.

Jim was offered two professional contracts: with Aston Martin in Formula 1, alongside Roy Salvadori and Maurice Trintignant, and with Team Lotus in Formula Junior and Formula 2. After typical deliberation, and much urging from Scott-Watson and McBain, he decided to accept both: "To give motor racing a real try," he said. He appointed a manager for the farm and became a professional racing driver. He was 22.

BELOW Jim contested 15 races, plus sprints and hillclimbs, with this Porsche 356 over three of his formative seasons. Here, he monsters Ted Lund's MGA Twin-Cam at Charterhall in 1958. Formerly owned by Bill Cotton, the racing band leader, this 1600cc, 100mph car delivered Jim's first track racing victory, at Charterhall in October 1957. He grew to love the 1600S and bought it when Ian Scott-Watson replaced it with a Lotus Elan in 1959. Ultimately it clocked up more than 80,000 miles.

LEFT Jim tentatively climbs aboard the Border Reivers' newly acquired, three-year-old 3.4-litre Jaguar D Type for a test at Charterhall, encouraged by Jock McBain and Ian Scott-Watson.

ABOVE Grappling with the Border Reivers' D Type Jaguar at Charterhall in 1958. Jim did 18 British club races with this car, which had previously been driven by such as Archie Scott-Brown and Henry Taylor. He won 11 of them and thought it "a bit of a lark" trailing it to meetings behind Ian Scott-Watson's Ford Thames van, staying in local B&Bs and hotels, wooing the prettiest girls, and then beating up the opposition. Note the Border Reivers horseman emblem on the front wing.

ABOVE Jim's performances here at Crimond inspired the Border Reivers to take both their cars to the 1958 sports car Grand Prix meeting at Spa-Francorchamps in May – Jim's first National or International event. He drove the 1600S Porsche brilliantly in the 2-litre race, holding second place before having to give way to more powerful cars on a drying track. The 130-mile, International-status main event included Archie Scott-Brown, Masten Gregory, Bruce Halford and Peter Whitehead in Lister-Jaguars, Carroll Shelby and Paul Frère in works Aston Martin DBR2s, Olivier Gendebien and Lucien Bianchi in Ferrari Testa Rossas, Franco Bordoni and Antonio Negri in works Maserati 200Ss, and Ivor Bueb and Jack Fairman in D Types. Jim finished eighth, but not without a big scare, recovering a 175mph slide in the Masta Kink when foolhardily trying to stay with the leaders. 'Autosport' readers were kept well informed: team manager Ian Scott-Watson wrote the Spa report, but had to return to the UK before the racing on Sunday. Jim therefore 'phoned through the details, making sure the readers knew all about his speed in the rain!
(Photo courtesy of Graham Gauld)

RIGHT Having owned two Sunbeam Talbots and a Triumph TR2, Jim bought this TR3A as his personal transport in 1958 and entered it in a number of Scottish rallies, sprints and hillclimbs. Navigated by a grain merchant friend, Andrew Russell, he used this car to win the Border Rally, a round of the Scottish Rally Championship. Two years after his death, in 1970, this event was renamed in his honour by friends including members of the Berwick & District Motor Club, of which he had been the president. It became Britain's first stage rally on closed public roads and, in 1999, a round of the British Championship. Since 2003, it has been included in the Irish Tarmac Championship and is one of the biggest motorsport events in the UK.
(Photo courtesy of Graham Gauld)

LEFT The GT race at the Boxing Day Brands Hatch meeting, 1958. Jim and Ian Scott-Watson caught the sleeper from Edinburgh to London on Christmas night, picked up a new Lotus Elite from the Green Park Hotel on Boxing Day morning, drove it to Kent, stuck numbers on it, and went racing. Jim qualified on an all-Elite front row alongside Colin Chapman himself and Mike Costin – and, after a brief battle, pulled away from them both. Just before the end of the race, Jim was clipped when lapping an Austin-Healey Sprite here at the Druids hairpin, and Chapman (following) went past to win. But the founder and the designer of Team Lotus, which had entered Formula 1 earlier in the year, were both profoundly impressed. Chapman invited him on the spot to join Team Lotus, but Jim felt unready to take up racing as a profession.

ABOVE Jim steadily built up self-confidence as a racing driver in 1959 with the Border Reivers' Lister-Jaguar sports-racing car, previously raced by Bruce Halford. He is pictured at Aintree during the International 200 meeting that April, engaged in a duel with Graham Whitehead. The Aston Martin DBR1 passed the Lister before the end to finish fifth behind Roy Salvadori (Cooper), Graham Hill (Lotus) and Ecurie Ecosse drivers Masten Gregory (Lister) and Ron Flockhart (Tojeiro). Exalted company…

LEFT The scene in a rented garage near Le Mans in June 1959 as the works Team Lotus mechanics prepare the works Elite that was to be raced in the 24 Hours under the Border Reivers banner, although overseen by Colin Chapman himself. Jim (at left) has found a French admirer. At right (white shirt), Ian Scott-Watson is deciding to buy the car for the Border Reivers programme.

LEFT Jim corners his Lotus Elite at Le Mans in 1959. His progress with co-driver John Whitmore was hampered by a faulty starter motor but they finished the race, 10th overall and second in their class behind another Elite driven by Peter Lumsden and Peter Riley. Jim disliked his first Le Mans experience, alarmed by the wide variances in driving ability.

ABOVE Jim's career reached what he himself recognised as a turning point one day in August 1959. David Murray invited him to do the big Tourist Trophy sports car race at Goodwood, co-driving the Ecurie Ecosse Tojeiro-Jaguar with Masten Gregory – one of Jim's personal racing heroes. Gregory (pictured at left, lapping a Lotus 11) was no quicker than Jim all weekend, and crashed the car out of the race, claiming a brake failure. The experience, said Jim, "had a profound effect on me, [because] I realised that I might seriously compete with the idols of my schooldays".

RIGHT Jim is congratulated by (left to right) race reporter David Pritchard, 'Autosport' editor Gregor Grant, photojournalist Max Le Grand, Ian Scott-Watson and journalist Roger Willis, after an immaculate victory in the 1959 'Autosport' 3 Hours day-and-night race at Snetterton. He started his Lotus Elite from pole position ahead of Dick Protheroe's Jaguar and Gawaine Baillie's Corvette, and won the 30-car race by more than two laps at an average speed of almost 80mph. The win made him the 1600cc class champion in that year's 'Autosport' Production Sports Car series, one of four class titles he won that season. In both 1958 and 1959, Jim was declared as the Scottish Speed Champion.

BELOW Jim had his very first single-seater race at the end of 1959, back at Brands Hatch to race the Elan in the Boxing Day meeting. The car was a front-engined Gemini, built by Chequered Flag founder Graham Warner (with whom Jim had had many dices that season in their Lotus Elites) and named after his star sign. The event was the first ever Formula Junior race. Pictured following one of the new, mid-engined Coopers, driven by Ian Burgess, Jim did not enjoy the outing, hampered by a weak battery and soaked by drizzle. Another new mid-engined car made its début in this race: an unpainted, prototype Lotus 18 Climax, driven by works driver Alan Stacey.

1960

INTO THE BIG TIME
WITH TEAM LOTUS

In January, Jim Clark had the prospect of a maiden Formula 1 season with Aston Martin, but he never raced the car. Early in the final season of the 2.5-litre formula, it was clear that the front-engined DBR5 was uncompetitive with the Ferrari 246 and BRM P25, let alone the nimble, mid-engined Cooper T51 and Lotus 18. The new team started only one race before David Brown cancelled his company's programme. After strong performances for Team Lotus in Formula Junior and Formula 2, alongside Trevor Taylor and the senior works drivers, Innes Ireland, Alan Stacey and John Surtees, Jim was drafted into the Formula 1 effort. This first season as a professional was also the first in his enduring relationship with Colin Chapman. Together, they would transform Lotus into a world-beating Grand Prix team.

RIGHT The start of something big: Jim Clark's Formula 1 début at Zandvoort in June 1960, when he stood in for Team Lotus driver John Surtees, who had a clashing motorcycle race. Jim's Lotus 18 is pictured early in the Dutch Grand Prix, chasing Tony Brooks's Yeoman Credit Cooper T51 through the Hunzerug corner behind the pits and up the slope into the sand dunes.

LEFT Jim's first race as a works driver was the Formula Junior event in March 1960 at Goodwood, where he secured the first victory for a Lotus 18 and for a Cosworth engine. The performance spoiled John Surtees's racing début on four wheels: the multiple motorcycling champion, driving Ken Tyrrell's BMC powered Cooper Mk1, eventually finished 3sec behind. Team Lotus, also represented by Trevor Taylor and Peter Arundell, was virtually unbeatable in Formula Junior in 1960, winning 19 races including nine 1–2 finishes, one of which (at Oulton Park) hugely impressed a young spectator named Jackie Stewart. Jim won seven times in England and once in Germany, at Solitude.

ABOVE Jim's first Formula 2 race, with Team Lotus on the Heysel street circuit for the Brussels Grand Prix in April 1960, pitched him for the first time among front-running Grand Prix drivers. He was quicker than both his senior team mates, Alan Stacey and Innes Ireland, qualifying fifth behind Jo Bonnier and Stirling Moss in Porsches, Chris Bristow in a Yeoman Credit Cooper and the eventual winner, Jack Brabham in a works Cooper. Pictured dicing with the Centro-Sud and Yeoman Credit Coopers of Maurice Trintignant and Harry Schell, who are *en route* to second and third, Jim was stopped by a broken engine. This was Schell's penultimate race: he lost his life in qualifying for the International Trophy at Silverstone four weeks later.

RIGHT Stirling Moss prided himself on being virtually unbeatable in Le Mans-style echelon starts but here, at the Nürburgring for the ADAC 1000-kilometre race, he has been beaten in the sprint across the track by a young upstart. Moss, in the white Maserati (No 5), is looking over his left shoulder as he realises that Jim was first in the cockpit of his Aston Martin (No 8) and is on the move a fraction of a second before him. The two are leaving behind the Porsche RS60s of pole man Jo Bonnier and Hans Herrmann, and the Ferrari Testa Rossas of Phil Hill and Richie Ginther.

ABOVE Jim leads Stirling through the South Turn on the opening lap of the 67-car Nürburgring 1000km. The Border Reivers' Aston Martin DBR1/300 was an ex-works car that had been all but burned out in a fire during the previous year's Tourist Trophy at Goodwood. It was no match for the Camoradi team's 'birdcage' Maserati. Moss was soon in the lead, and pulling away to win the race with co-driver Dan Gurney. Clark was also passed by Jo Bonnier (Porsche), Phil Hill (Ferrari) and Masten Gregory in the other Camoradi Maserati. He repassed Gregory but his engine broke early in the sixth lap, leaving his co-driver, Roy Salvadori, without any work that day.

RIGHT Here is the start of Jim's almost unbelievable run of bad luck in Monte Carlo. His works Lotus 18 was a full second quickest in qualifying for the Formula Junior race at the end of May, and here he takes the lead, flanked by team mate Trevor Taylor and trailed by Peter Arundell in another Lotus, Peter Ashdown (Lola) and Kurt Lincoln in the white Cooper. Jim left them all behind and was leading the race by 10 seconds when, shortly before the end, he was stymied by an ignition fault. Henry Taylor (Cooper) won, and Jim's Lotus spluttered across the line in seventh place.

LEFT Jim at speed on his Formula 1 début in the Dutch Grand Prix. He qualified 11th of the 17 starters, beaten this time by team mates Innes Ireland and Alan Stacey, but moved up the order on race day until he encountered Graham Hill's fourth-placed BRM P48. With Jim's team mates almost in view ahead on the track, they duelled for more than 30 laps until Jim's gearbox broke after 41 of the 75 laps. A transmission failure also accounted for Stacey, and it was Ireland who finished second to Jack Brabham's works Cooper T53, with Hill third.

ABOVE Jim exits the La Source hairpin at Spa-Francorchamps during his second Grand Prix, a fortnight after Zandvoort. Spa was one of three of the season's Formula 1 venues on which he had raced before – the day Archie Scott-Brown had been killed in 1958. On this occasion, Stirling Moss broke both legs in a 130mph accident in practice, caused by a hub failure on Rob Walker's Lotus 18. On race day, Chris Bristow lost control of his Yeoman Credit Cooper in trying to pass Willy Mairesse's Ferrari, and was killed. Then Jim's team mate, Alan Stacey, was struck in the face by a bird, and he was killed, too. Jim picked up his first World Championship points score, but his fifth place was joyless. He had been the first on the scene of Bristow's accident and, after the finish, he noticed that his Lotus was spattered with blood. "If any one race gave me thoughts of retiring," he said, "it was this one."

LEFT Jim went straight from the infamous 1960 Belgian Grand Prix to Le Mans for a date with Border Reivers, which had entered its blue Aston Martin DBR1 in the 24-hour race. The car had been prepared by the works mechanics in Feltham and the team brought along an enthusiastic troupe of Scottish farmers as its pit crew. Here Jim swings the car through the Esses, *en route* to third place with his accomplished co-driver, Roy Salvadori. Jim had established the Aston as a contender while it was raining early in the race, and it was the only non-Ferrari to finish the great race among the top seven.

ABOVE Jim heads for the best result of his maiden Formula 1 season on the street circuit at Porto, where he amazed himself by finishing third in the Portuguese Grand Prix behind the works Coopers of Jack Brabham and Bruce McLaren. Jim was third fastest in the first session, but then tried a new line through one of the turns. It sent his Lotus 18 skidding into a kerb and through a strawbale barrier, trashing its front end. Team owner Colin Chapman and chief mechanic Jim Endruweit personally worked all night with an oxy-acetylene torch to remove the bent frame tubes and replace them with pieces cut from quick-lift jacks. Finally they patched up the nosecone glassfibre with several rolls of white tape. Jim took up eighth position on the grid as a 'starting money special', but was told to keep going if the car felt OK. Attrition ahead put him on the podium, but this success was the last thing on his mind as he stopped the car: he had eaten something bad on race morning, and had to flee to the nearest lavatory.

PREVIOUS PAGE Jim was robbed of his first Formula 2 victory when the Solitude circuit, near Stuttgart, was used in July for the first time for a big race since 1950. He was dominating from pole there when a blown head gasket intervened, so he had to wait five more weeks and his fourth race in the category, the Kentish 100 at Brands Hatch. Having qualified fourth, he is pictured (at right) trailing Dan Gurney in American entrant Louise Bryden-Brown's Lotus 18 (partially visible at far left), Innes Ireland (whose works Lotus has jumped the start from the second row) and Stirling Moss in Rob Walker's Porsche, and under pressure from Graham Hill's works Porsche.

ABOVE Jim's face is a picture of concentration as he takes the 1.5-litre Lotus 18 out of Stirling's Bend, on the brand new Grand Prix loop at Brands Hatch, and on to an epic victory in the Kentish 100. Jim fought a long battle for the lead with John Surtees and Dan Gurney in two more Lotus 18s and the works Porsches of Graham Hill and Jo Bonnier. He held off a late charge from Gurney to win by 0.4sec, with Bonnier third, Hill fourth, and Surtees's works Lotus parked with broken suspension after a collision with fellow bike racer Geoff Duke.

RIGHT Jim gets the bubbly after his first Formula 2 victory. Having won the Brands Hatch feature event, he finished second in the Formula Junior race behind team mate Trevor Taylor, despite falling to the very back of the field after a first-lap incident.

ABOVE Jim lost the lead of the non-championship Lombank Trophy Formula 1 race at Snetterton in September when he missed his braking point at the Esses and slithered into the escape road there, allowing Innes Ireland past him to head an eventual Team Lotus 1–2. Ireland didn't care how wins came to him. Here he celebrates in characteristic style with Jim (who drank rarely) and his great friend from the Borders, Ian Scott-Watson. Ireland later became resentful of Clark's success and although Jim, for the most part, shrugged it off, there was an 'incident' at Monza in 1962 when Ireland, a lap behind, made life difficult for his younger compatriate. Scott-Watson, meanwhile, kept in touch with Jim right through to the end, often meeting his 'protégé' for dinner in London even in the late 1960s.

RIGHT Disappointment for Jim in the final championship race for the 2.5-litre Formula 1. He qualified fifth for the US Grand Prix at Riverside, California, just ahead of team mates John Surtees and Innes Ireland, but was taken out on the fourth lap when Surtees tried to go round the outside of him and lost it on the 'marbles'. Jimmy's Lotus 18 rammed its broadside sister car (which was out on the spot) and he spent the rest of the race in and out of the pits, finishing 16th and last. Ireland went on to finish second behind Stirling Moss in Rob Walker's Lotus.

1 9 6 1

JOY IN PAU, BUT HORROR IN ITALY

Before the inaugural 1.5-litre Formula 1 World Championship, Jim raced for the first time outside Europe when Team Lotus sent 2.5-litre 'Intercontinental Formula' cars to New Zealand in January. Thereafter he confined himself to Formula 1, teamed with Innes Ireland and Trevor Taylor and armed with the new Lotus 21, and outings in Aston Martin sports cars. April brought his first Formula 1 victory, in the Grand Prix de Pau, but the championship events were mostly dominated by the 'sharknose' Ferrari 156, and Jim did not lead a single lap all year. Instead, he had to remember this season for a dreadful experience at Monza. Wolfgang von Trips was headed for the title when his Ferrari touched wheels with Jim's Lotus under braking. Trips was killed in the ensuing accident, and so were 14 spectators.

RIGHT Jim got right among the 'sharknose' V6 Ferraris at Zandvoort, and engaged Phil Hill in a long duel over second place behind Wolfgang von Trips. Hill did eventually complete the anticipated Ferrari 1–2 but this was an exceptionally tenacious performance by Jim with an inferior car. He said of it: "A lot of people began to take notice of me after that drive."

LEFT Jim's maiden Formula 1 victory came early in his second season, in his 11th such event. There were clashing non-championship races on Easter Monday, and Team Lotus split its effort, sending Innes Ireland and Henry Taylor to Goodwood for the International 100, and Jim and Trevor Taylor to south-west France for the Pau Grand Prix. Cooper did likewise and, in the absence of the more powerful cars from Ferrari and Porsche, Jim was outpaced in qualifying here only by Jack Brabham. But he managed to grab the lead at the start, and was still there when the defending World Champion's Cooper was halted by a broken fuel pump. Late in the race Jim also ran short of fuel, obliging him to display yet again his amazing ability to drive around a problem. On this occasion he reduced revs and used longer gears. Pictured completing his slowdown lap, he won easily from Jo Bonnier in a similar, Scuderia Colonia Lotus 18. This was the first of his 48 Formula 1 victories in total.

LEFT Ferrari and Porsche both sent cars to Sicily in late April for the non-championship race on the Syracuse circuit, where Formula 1 débutant Giancarlo Baghetti famously won in his red car, with the Porsches second and third. Even the Mk2 version of the Coventry Climax FPF in-line four gave about 40bhp to the V6 Ferrari and 10bhp to the Porsche flat-four. The works Lotuses were particularly uncompetitive here, bottoming alarmingly when filled with fuel. The last time in a Formula 1 Lotus 18, Jim drove a cautious race, although he did pass Lorenzo Bandini in the Centro Sud team's Cooper-Maserati (leading him here) to take sixth place.

ABOVE The début of the Lotus 21, in the opening 1961 championship race in Monte Carlo. Jim went fastest in the Thursday qualifying but then crashed heavily, as did team mate Innes Ireland, who broke a leg. Jim's car was repaired and here, just after the start, he leads pole man Stirling Moss in Rob Walker's now outdated Lotus 18 and Dan Gurney and Jo Bonnier in Porsches in pursuit of Richie Ginther's Ferrari. A broken ignition lead sent Jim to the pits on the second lap and it was left to Moss to take the fight to Ferrari, which he did brilliantly.

ABOVE Jim agreed to drive in sportscar racing this season for John Ogier, a wealthy Essex chicken farmer. Here he corners the Essex Racing Aston Martin DBR1 during his first race with it, the ADAC 1000km on the Nürburgring, where he was co-driven by Bruce McLaren. For the second year running, Jim outsprinted Stirling Moss in the Le Mans start but was passed by Moss (this time at the wheel of a Porsche RS61) during the opening lap. The Aston was clearly inferior to the Porsches, Ferraris and Maseratis, but Jim was holding down fourth place when an oil line ruptured after 25 of the 44 laps.

RIGHT Jim returned to the Border Reivers for the Le Mans 24 Hours, in which their Aston Martin DBR1, third the previous June, was co-driven by Ron Flockhart, Ecurie Ecosse's 1956–57 race winner. Yet again Jim was first on the move at the echelon start but he was swamped by six of the much faster Ferraris along the 3.5 miles of the Mulsanne Straight. He is pictured leading Roy Salvadori, driving John Ogier's DBR1, into Tertre Rouge corner. During the fourth hour, the boot lid blew off Jim's car, but he and Flockhart had established a solid seventh place when, at 2.45am, the clutch exploded while Jim was speeding down that awesome straight.

OPPOSITE TOP After practice for the Belgian Grand Prix at Spa-Francorchamps, Jim is the only man standing in an apparently relaxed meeting of the new Grand Prix Drivers Association, formed in the Metropole Hotel on the Thursday at Monaco the month before. They are discussing the implications of an accident at Blanchimont involving the UDT-Laystall team's Lotus 18, in which Cliff Allison had suffered career-ending injuries. All the drivers had stopped at the scene, where they had waited 15 minutes for an ambulance to arrive. Also identifiably involved are (left to right) Jack Brabham, Innes Ireland, Masten Gregory, Bruce McLaren, Jo Bonnier, Stirling Moss (the first GPDA president), Richie Ginther, Phil Hill and Dan Gurney. British journalist Peter Garnier, taking the minutes as the secretary (and treasurer) of the new group, wears his trademark sports jacket.

ABOVE On a blistering hot day in Reims, Team Lotus has Giancarlo Baghetti in its grip early in the French Grand Prix, but Ferrari's fourth driver went on to an epic victory. Baghetti's team mates dominated the action but Wolfgang von Trips and Richie Ginther suffered mechanical failures and Phil Hill spun away the lead here at the Thillois hairpin, and stalled. Baghetti held off Dan Gurney's Porsche to win his first World Championship race. Jim, leading here, was racing them both when his goggles were smashed by a hail of stones from the disintegrating track surface. In putting on his spare goggles, he dropped out of the slipstream and finished third, his face covered in blood (and his right foot badly burned by the overheated pedals). Strangely, it was also at Reims in 1966 that Jim suffered another bloody goggles incident: on this occasion he was hit by a bird in practice. Jim was very lucky not to be seriously injured by the shattered lenses, but missed the race nonetheless. Innes Ireland was fourth with more stones jamming his throttle slides.

OPPOSITE BOTTOM The week after Reims, Jim dragged his burned foot into an 'Intercontinental Formula' Lotus 18 (powered by a 2.5-litre former Formula 1 Climax engine) for the British Empire Trophy race at Silverstone. This duel with Tony Brooks was resolved when the BRM broke a valve spring. Jim finished in a painful fifth position in a race dominated by Stirling Moss in Rob Walker's Cooper-Climax.

LEFT Jim, lined up in seventh position on the starting grid at Aintree. After the start, the handling of the Lotus 21 made the most of Dunlop's brand-new, high-hysteris rain tyres. Jim went fifth early on but, when the rain stopped, he fell back again. With 13 laps remaining, his lap and upper body were suddenly covered with hot engine oil when the cockpit pressure gauge burst...

ABOVE All the fun of the fair at Solitude in southern Germany, a week after the British Grand Prix and only two before the German. A group of Formula 1 people, perched on a wagon behind a tractor driven by Porsche works driver Jo Bonnier, arrives for a party thrown by Porsche after practice. Trevor Taylor and Innes Ireland are standing at the back, the latter steadied by the hand of Hans Herrmann. Among the others seated are Colin Chapman, Michael May and Jim Clark.

ABOVE Team Lotus had a great day at Solitude. In a very tight finish, Innes Ireland gave Colin Chapman's team a much-needed boost by beating the Porsches of Jo Bonnier and Dan Gurney on their home turf, and Trevor Taylor and Pete Arundell finished 1–2 in the Formula Junior race. For an off-form Jim (pictured), it was a less happy weekend. Before flying to Germany, he had set out to drive from Liverpool home to Duns, and had been involved in a nasty road accident in northern Lancashire. He had been shaken by the incident and needed stitches in a head wound. Not the best July he ever had...

LEFT A Dunlop group photograph at the Nürburgring where the tyre company, in its fourth Formula 1 season, won its 30th Grand Prix (with Stirling Moss). Jim and Lotus team mate Innes Ireland are joking with rival entrant John Cooper, while Jack Brabham is talking with Moss, Graham Hill and Jo Bonnier have bagged the only seats, and Bruce McLaren and Dan Gurney stand at right. Dunlop's competition director, Dick Jeffrey, stands modestly behind the group (in jacket and tie, between Bonnier and McLaren).

ABOVE The wrecks of Jim's Lotus and 'Taffy' von Trips's Ferrari after the appalling accident during the Italian Grand Prix that killed the German driver and 14 Monza spectators. Clark made a great start in the Italian Grand Prix, Trips a poor one from pole position. On the second lap, Trips surged past Graham Hill's BRM into fifth place, then Jim's Lotus into fourth, whereupon he got out of shape under braking and touched wheels with Jim. The Ferrari cartwheeled into the crowd and back onto the track again. The Lotus also overturned, but Jim was uninjured. "I felt sick through and through," Jim said. "One minute I was enjoying the racing, and the next I was walking away from a ghastly mess. I was deeply depressed." The incident, which effectively handed the World Championship to Phil Hill, plagued Jim and Team Lotus for years afterwards as the Italian authorities tried to find someone to blame.

RIGHT Jim indulges in a full-blooded drift at Goodwood during the Tourist Trophy, first-time-out in an Aston Martin DB4GT, one of three entered by John Ogier. This race was won by Stirling Moss in Rob Walker's Ferrari 250GT, with Mike Parkes second in another Ferrari. Despite unsurprisingly excessive tyre wear, however, the Aston Martins won the team prize in finishing 3–4–5, Roy Salvadori and Jim in Zagato-bodied cars ahead of Innes Ireland in a regular DB4.

LEFT Jim went to Watkins Glen for the US Grand Prix still downcast after the fatalities at Monza four weeks before, and his nerves were put on the edge when team mate Innes Ireland's steering broke during practice. On race day, a broken oil seal, causing a slipping clutch, ruined his run into a distant seventh place. With one of its drivers dead and the Italian media at its throat (and both titles won), Ferrari did not do the final round. In defeating Dan Gurney's Porsche, therefore, Ireland picked up the win after Stirling Moss (Lotus), Jack Brabham (Cooper) and Graham Hill (BRM) had all run into trouble, thus becoming the first Scot to win a World Championship event. Shortly afterwards, nevertheless, Ireland was controversially dropped by Team Lotus, and Jimmy promoted to the No 1 status. Colin Chapman had seen the future.

ABOVE Shameful ribaldry during the West Essex Car Club dinner-dance in mid-November as MC John Trimble invites Jim to down an evidently highly suspicious 'Laird's Mix', watched by (left to right) Peter Jopp, Graham Hill and Ron Flockhart.

LEFT Jim celebrated his new status at Team Lotus in the Springbox Series in South Africa in December 1961, where four races were held in four weeks. With the tragedy of Monza still relatively recent history, these non-championship races proved to be a welcome distraction and enabled Stirling Moss to introduce Jim to water-skiing. Jim won the first three races (Kyalami, Durban and East London) from pole and finished second to his friend and team-mate, Trevor Taylor, at Killarney after a loose oil line sprayed fluid onto the rear wheels and caused him to spin. Here, with the side panels of his Lotus 21 removed on a sweltering Boxing Day, he heads for victory in the South African Grand Prix at East London – a momentous occasion because Jim lost 15 seconds when he spun to avoid Dave Wright's stationary Cooper and then regained all that ground and more to beat none other than arch-rival Moss by 17sec.

1 9 6 2

A TITLE LOST IN THE FINAL ROUND

Colin Chapman and Team Lotus transformed racecar engineering over the winter of 1961–62 with the first aluminium monocoque Formula 1 car, the Lotus 25, powered by the new Coventry Climax V8. The chassis was much more rigid than the old-style tubular frames and the 25 was a perfect tool for Jim, whose uncanny precision was already a hallmark. With Innes Ireland dropped, he was now the team's No 1 driver, teamed with Trevor Taylor. The new car was not reliable but it delivered his first three victories in the World Championship, putting him in contention for the title. It went to the wire in South Africa between him and Graham Hill. From his sixth pole position of the season, Jim led 63 of the 82 laps, but was halted by an oil leak. The BRM driver went on to win the race, and the main prize.

RIGHT Jim achieves his maiden World Championship victory – and the first of four consecutively at Spa, a circuit he detested. A stripped timing gear left him 12th on the grid but he risked all at the start, grabbing fifth place. As others faltered, he was leading from Trevor Taylor and Ferrari's Willy Mairesse when they crashed, and won easily from BRM's Graham Hill.

ABOVE Before the World Championship began, Jim did five Formula 1 races with the Climax V8 powered Lotus 24, winning the Lombank Trophy at Snetterton and the BARC 200 at Aintree (pictured), but famously losing out to Graham Hill in a photo-finish in the International Trophy race at Silverstone, having led all the way. The rivals of Team Lotus did not know that the spaceframe 24 was only an interim car.

RIGHT The Lotus 25 is a snug fit. Powered by the new Coventry Climax V8, the first monocoque Formula 1 car was effective straight away, much to the dismay of customers who had purchased 24s. Contrary to popular belief, Jim took a while to get used to the laydown driving position, which was much more pronounced than in the 21 and 24, and required a lot of reorientation with racing lines.

LEFT The début of the Lotus 25 came in the opening World Championship race at Zandvoort. On the first lap, Jim is leading at the Tarzan hairpin, pursued by Graham Hill (BRM P57), Dan Gurney (Porsche 804), pole man John Surtees (Lola Mk4), Bruce McLaren (Cooper T60, almost out of shot), Phil Hill (Ferrari 156), Innes Ireland (Lotus 24), Ricardo Rodriguez (Ferrari), Jack Brabham (inside line) and Trevor Taylor (Lotus 24s), Giancarlo Baghetti (Ferrari), Masten Gregory (Lotus 18/21), Jo Bonnier (Porsche) and Tony Maggs (Cooper T55).

ABOVE This was an imperfect début of the Lotus 25 – and a sign of things to come. Jim led the Dutch Grand Prix until a malfunctioning clutch overheated the gearbox and he had to pit, eventually resuming to finish ninth. Graham Hill won the race for BRM with Jim's team mate, Trevor Taylor, in second place with a Lotus 24.

RIGHT Here aiming his Lotus 25 for the apex in Casino Square, Jim qualified on pole position in Monaco, 0.4sec clear of Graham Hill's BRM, but fell to seventh place in first-corner mayhem caused by Willy Mairesse's recklessly driven Ferrari. By hunting down and overtaking in turn the Ferraris of Lorenzo Bandini and Phil Hill, Jack Brabham's Lotus 24 and Bruce McLaren's Cooper, Jim retrieved second place behind the BRM on the 27th lap, but the clutch malfunctioned again and caused an engine blow-up 30 laps later. Hill's V8 faltered near the end, and it was McLaren who won.

ABOVE Jim startled his own team, not to mention Ferrari and Porsche, in the ADAC 1000km. The lightweight Lotus 23 sports-racer, powered by a 1500cc, 95bhp Ford in-line four with an experimental twin-cam cylinder head developed by Lotus, was finished in the Nürburgring paddock the day before the race. Jim had a great start – and built a 25sec lead at the end of the opening lap. At 11 laps, quarter-distance, he was still leading with ease (and disbelief) when he was all but overcome by fumes from a leaking exhaust, missed a shift, and crashed. Ferrari inherited a 1–2, with Porsche third. The following month, the works Lotus was controversially declared "unsafe" by the scrutineers at Le Mans: the company never again entered the 24 Hours, and neither did Jim.

RIGHT The winners of the first three races in the 1962 World Championship shared the front row at Rouen-les-Essarts, with Jim (at left) on pole, more than 7sec under the 2.5-litre lap record, and Graham Hill (BRM P57) and Bruce McLaren (Cooper T60) alongside him. At the start of the French Grand Prix, Hill took the lead and Jim, hampered by a slight misfire, was passed by John Surtees's Bowmaker-Yeoman Lola Mk4. Later Hill and Surtees were both delayed and Jim led, only to retire due to a suspension failure. Dan Gurney (Porsche 804) made it four winners in four races.

LEFT Jim shares a joke with Graham Hill in the pit-lane at Rouen-les-Essarts during the French Grand Prix meeting. After Spa, they have one win each and Graham, leading Phil Hill and Jim 16–14–9 in the World Championship, now understands the potential of the Lotus 25. With Ferrari fading, the BRM driver is beginning to realise that Jim is his main rival for the title.

ABOVE Jim displays the precision for which he was already famous as he corners his Lotus 25 at Aintree. It all came together for Team Lotus in the British Grand Prix. After shaking off a brisk early challenge from John Surtees's Lola, Jim led the entire distance from pole position, driving the fastest lap for good measure. Surtees was half a minute behind at the finish, ahead of Bruce McLaren's Cooper. Jim began 1962 with a white peak on his Everoak helmet, but discarded it for the next 18 months (Monaco aside) when it blew off on the back straight at Spa!

LEFT Watched by the big Aintree crowd, Jim receives his British Grand Prix trophy after an impressive victory that put him firmly into contention for the championship. Graham Hill's fourth place for BRM kept him tenuously in the lead of the points table, with 19 to Jim's 18.

LEFT Jim and Colin Chapman accepted with alacrity when the Team Lotus No 1 was invited to try Lorenzo Bandini's brand new Ferrari 156 for size in the Nürburgring paddock. Fierce internal politics at Maranello, leading to a walkout by the team's top engineers the previous winter, had blunted Ferrari's efforts this season. After the German and Italian Grands Prix, Ferrari pulled out of the championship, citing "labour problems". On the wet race day here, Jim was so preoccupied with clearing his misted-up goggles that he forgot to switch on the Bendix fuel pumps. His engine died as he left the grid, and the whole field went by. Furious with himself, he drove a brilliant race to fourth place behind Graham Hill's BRM, John Surtees's Lola and Dan Gurney's Porsche.

ABOVE One of the most embarrassing moments of Jim's career came during the 1962 Tourist Trophy at Goodwood, in which he again raced John Ogier's Aston Martin DB4GT Zagato. He made another terrific start but his car was way off the Ferrari 250GTO pace, and he was soon in sixth place, fighting skittish handling in the faster turns. Just after half-distance, he spotted John Surtees coming up to lap him with the Bowmaker-run GTO. Trying to get out of the way of the race leader, Jim spun, and Surtees could not avoid a collision. Both cars ended in the ditch and Innes Ireland, Graham Hill and Mike Parkes took the spoils with three more Ferraris.

ABOVE Jim was outqualified by Richie Ginther, in a works BRM, before the Oulton Park Gold Cup, but there was no beating him on race day. The Lotus 25 put half a second on the pursuit on every lap. Jim very nearly lapped Graham Hill in the second-placed P57, with Ginther gone due to an engine failure.

RIGHT The drivers' briefing at Monza. Left to right: Masten Gregory, Roy Salvadori, John Surtees, Carel de Beaufort, Tony Maggs, Innes Ireland, Graham Hill and Jim. Qualifying delivered another pole position for the Lotus 25 but a new gearbox, fitted overnight, began to seize soon after the start of the Italian Grand Prix. Hill and Richie Ginther achieved a 1–2 for BRM.

ABOVE Tex Hopkins waves the chequered flag at Jim in typically extravagant style at Watkins Glen. Jim, from another pole, lost the lead to Graham Hill for seven laps after being badly baulked by a backmarker, but repassed the BRM without undue difficulty, running out the winner by almost 9sec. The two of them lapped all the others and came away from upstate New York with Graham holding a nine-point lead. This season, only the best five scores were to be counted, and this meant that Jim would claim the title if he won in South Africa. The protagonists had to wait 12 weeks for the dénouement...

RIGHT The Formula 1 title contenders side-by-side at the front of the grid on the narrow East London circuit, with Jim's yellow-wheeled Lotus on pole position. Graham Hill had scored in seven of the season's eight races, amassing 43 points, whereas the fast but fragile Lotus had delivered only four scores for Jim, totalling 30 points. With the best five results to count, the nett scores were 39–30. Graham could only add to his total by winning, so a victory would do the job for Jimmy. The BRM was trailing the Lotus by half a minute after 60 of the 82 laps, and Graham thought the championship was lost. Then the Lotus let Jim down yet again. A dislodged plug caused an engine oil leak, and Jim parked it.

1 9 6 3

WORLD CHAMPION
FOR THE FIRST TIME

The new World Championship began with another disappointing non-finish for the Lotus team leader in Monaco, but then the 25 found reliability – and Jimmy, usually partnered by Trevor Taylor again, became virtually unbeatable. The season brought seven superb victories from 10 Grands Prix, with seven pole positions, and five fastest laps. Jim beat Graham Hill (BRM) and Richie Ginther (Ferrari) to the title by a 44-point margin, and also won five non-championship Formula 1 races. In May, Team Lotus forayed to Indianapolis and shook up the USAC establishment with Jim's second place, which he converted to a victory later in the season on the Milwaukee Mile. Jim also won races in Lotus sports-racing cars and his season total of 19 victories in Internationals gilded his status as a new global star.

RIGHT No other Formula 1 driver led even one lap during the month of June 1963. Jim raced his Lotus 25 exclusively at the front in the Belgian, Dutch and French Grands Prix, starting on pole here at Zandvoort and at Reims, and driving the fastest lap in all three. A fourth straight victory, in the British Grand Prix in mid-July, all but wrapped up the championship.

ABOVE Jimmy looks a little apprehensive as he sits for the first time in the cockpit of a Lotus 29, the 4.2-litre Ford V8 powered USAC single-seater in which he had been entered for his first Indianapolis 500. After Ford executives had listened to Dan Gurney, and watched Jim testing a Formula 1 Lotus 25 on the Speedway, Team Lotus had the company's full backing when it built three of these cars early in 1963, a second for Gurney and a third as a spare. Each was powered by an all-aluminium derivative of the stockblock Fairlane pushrod engine, fuelled via carburettors.

RIGHT After testing the new USAC Lotus at Indianapolis, Jim opened his 1963 programme with pole position for the Lombank Trophy here at Snetterton at the end of March, but his Lotus 25 lost in the rain on race day to an inspired Graham Hill in an updated BRM P57. Nevertheless, Jim gave notice of what was in store for his rivals before the World Championship began. With the 25, now equipped with a fuel-injected, short-stroke version of the Climax V8, he won three more non-championship Formula 1 races at Pau, Imola and Silverstone.

LEFT Jim, on pole position, has a hand aloft at Aintree, signalling that his Lotus 25 is stranded. The battery was flat and, after the field had departed, he was pushed into pit-lane. Jim had won the BARC 200 here the previous season, but he enjoyed this race even more. He took over team mate Trevor Taylor's car and repeatedly smashed the lap record in a tremendous drive into third place. Two weeks later, he won the International Trophy at Silverstone before flying to America to qualify for Indy.

ABOVE Jim returned from America for the opening World Championship race, the 100-lap Grand Prix of Europe in Monte Carlo. Pictured in Casino Square, he put his Lotus 25 on pole position, 0.7sec clear of Graham Hill. With a full fuel load, malfunctioning fuel breather pipes caused his engine to splutter unpredictably, and he lost out to Hill and Richie Ginther. But the problem eased as the race progressed, allowing him to pass both BRMs and take the lead on lap 18. He was more than 15sec to the good and cruising when, on lap 79, his gearlever jammed itself in neutral when the gearbox was in fourth. On arrival at the Gasometer hairpin, the car spun to a noisy and smoky halt. Hill began his title defence at the head of a BRM 1–2.

LEFT Four days after his disappointment in Monaco, Jim was making his début in the Indianapolis 500. Having qualified fifth at just under 150mph, he drove the first part of the race with circumspection, on the fringe of the top 10, but then inexorably moved towards the front. Team Lotus had a one-stop strategy, whereas the front-engined USAC 'roadsters' that dominated the entry had to make at least two. Dan Gurney, having survived a big practice accident, raced the 'spare' Lotus 29 but was delayed when his pitstop was bungled. Jim's (pictured) went smoothly and he emerged in second place behind Parnelli Jones, who had led almost all the way from pole position with J.C. Agajanian's Watson-Offenhauser. In the final stages, Jones ought to have been black-flagged with a smoky oil leak, but ran out a controversial winner by about 20sec.

LEFT Jim seems to be pleading with the photographer to get him out of there as he sploshes down the hill past the pits during a torrential downpour late in the Belgian Grand Prix. Jim's qualifying was hampered by gearbox problems but, from eighth on the grid, he made an astonishing start and led the field into Eau Rouge. Then the gearbox again started jumping out of top (fifth) gear, so he had to grip the lever, steering only with his left hand, on all the fast sections – including the 150mph Masta kink. He was relieved when a gearbox failure parked Graham Hill's BRM, leaving him totally unchallenged. He won by almost five minutes over Bruce McLaren's Cooper.

ABOVE Jim in conference with Peter Arundell and Cosworth's Keith Duckworth during the French Grand Prix meeting. Arundell was the dominant force for Team Lotus in Formula Junior in 1962–63, and was being given occasional Formula 1 drives this season. He was entered in a third 25 at Reims, alongside Jim and Trevor Taylor, but ended up doing only the Junior race, in which he was defeated by Denny Hulme's Brabham. Jim won the main event very easily, despite an intermittent misfire.

ABOVE Jim heads for another dominant victory, in the British Grand Prix at Silverstone. He had his fourth pole of the year but this one was under close challenge from Dan Gurney and Jack Brabham in Brabham BT7s and Graham Hill in the latest BRM P57. All three jumped him at the start, as did Bruce McLaren (Cooper T66). It took Jim four whole laps to gain the lead... The Brabhams were both halted by engine failures, and Jim's 26sec victory – with a viciously oversteering car – was over John Surtees's Ferrari 156. Note the orange goggle lenses – relatively unusual for Clark.

RIGHT To Colin Chapman, standing proudly on the victory trailer with Jim at Silverstone, has come the realisation that a Team Lotus driver is going to be the 1963 World Champion. The Silverstone result put Jim on 36 points and his nearest rival, BRM's Richie Ginther, on only 14.

OPPOSITE TOP Jim hurls a wallowing Ford Galaxie at the Grand Prix loop at Brands Hatch during the Molyslip Trophy race there on August Bank Holiday Monday. Wherever possible, Jim liked to accept drives in anything new to him, and this particular offer came from entrant Alan Brown. Jim is pictured leading Jack Sears in John Willment's similar car, shortly to depart the scene with a flat tyre, but destined to win that year's British Saloon Car Championship. Jim won the race from a squadron of the previously dominant 3.8 Jaguars, led by Graham Hill, Roy Salvadori and Mike Salmon. "I've satisfied my curiosity," Jim said afterwards, "and I'll probably never race one [of these] again." He was right.

OPPOSITE BOTTOM Jim picks up a right-hand-drive Ford Galaxie with Sally Stokes, who was his girlfriend for more than three years. They met in 1963 but drifted apart during 1966. Jim was unwilling to commit himself while working as a professional racing driver. The following year, Sally married a Dutch racing driver, Ed Swart, and today the couple live not far away from Dan and Evi Gurney in California.

ABOVE In August, Jim missed the Mediterranean Grand Prix at Enna to race one of the Lotus-Ford USAC cars on the historic Milwaukee Mile, and achieved the first American victory for a mid-engined car. Team mate Dan Gurney finished third behind AJ Foyt's Trevis-Offy 'roadster'. The following month, Foyt won when the establishment was again challenged by Team Lotus in the Trenton 200: Clark and Gurney qualified 1–2 and had started lapping the roadsters when they were both stopped by broken oil lines.
(Photo courtesy of Russ Lake)

LEFT Jim has clinched the Drivers' World Championship (and the Constructors' title for Team Lotus) with a comfortable victory at Monza, and has just completed a lap of honour with Colin Chapman perched on the engine cover and gripping the rollover bar. The joy was not long unbridled. As Jim emerged from the car, he was asked to sign a legal document in connection with the Wolfgang von Trips fatalities here two years before. The document was in Italian, and Jim refused to sign it until it had been translated. He was told that was impossible, and what should have been a celebration turned into a confrontation.

ABOVE Alongside his Formula 1 and USAC commitments to Team Lotus, Jim did half a dozen sportscar races in 1963 with a Lotus 23B, winning at Oulton Park (twice), at Crystal Palace and here at Snetterton. Driving one of three Normand Racing entries in Norfolk, alongside Mike Beckwith and Tony Hegbourne, he repeated his 1959 success in the 'Autosport' 3 Hours, defeating Mike Parkes's Ferrari 250GTO in the process. Alongside Jim at left is Roy Salvadori in Tommy Atkins's Cooper Monaco, which was leading when its engine blew.

BELOW Team Lotus entered Jimmy and Trevor Taylor for the British Saloon Car Championship event supporting the annual three-hour race at Snetterton, equipping each with the newly launched Lotus Cortina. They staged a dead-heat for second place overall, humbled only by Jack Brabham in Alan Brown's huge Ford Galaxie. In all, Jim would do 22 races with Lotus Cortinas, winning eight of them outright against powerful V8 opposition, and securing 15 class victories. Jim thoroughly enjoyed racing these cars. He got a lot of fun out of it, and so did the British spectators.

RIGHT Jim stayed in North America in the three-week gap between the Formula 1 races at Watkins Glen and Mexico City to do the big West Coast sports car races at Riverside and Laguna Seca. He finished fifth at Riverside with a 1.6-litre Lotus 23B, winning the 2-litre division, and then did the Pacific Grand Prix with Frank Arciero's Lotus 19 (pictured). USRRC road racing was dominated by big V8s but, although equipped with a 2.7-litre Climax, Jim led this race. But the car's oil cooler was ruptured when Jim clipped a dislodged corner marker tyre, and Dave MacDonald drove past to repeat his Riverside victory with Shelby American's 'King Cobra' Cooper-Ford. Jim has just passed Walt Hansgen in Briggs Cunningham's Kjell Qvale built Genie.

ABOVE Jim gets his rear wheels spinning to beat John Surtees, in the monocoque Ferrari that had débuted at Monza, off the line at the start of the first World Championship race in Mexico City. The title had long been clinched, but Jim rubbed it in with a sixth victory, again leading every lap from pole position and setting the fastest lap. Surtees was disqualified for a push-start in pit-lane, and Jack Brabham was second ahead of the BRMs.

RIGHT A new force has come along to challenge the Lotus 25, in the shape of the Brabham BT7. Jim narrowly secured pole position for the season-closing South African Grand Prix at East London, flanked by Jack Brabham and Dan Gurney, with the Ferraris of John Surtees and Lorenzo Bandini behind. Again he led all the way, but Gurney drove the fastest lap *en route* to second place. This seventh victory in a single season (of 10 Grands Prix) broke a record that had been held jointly by Juan Manuel Fangio and Alberto Ascari and elevated Jim to a position amongst the all-time greats.

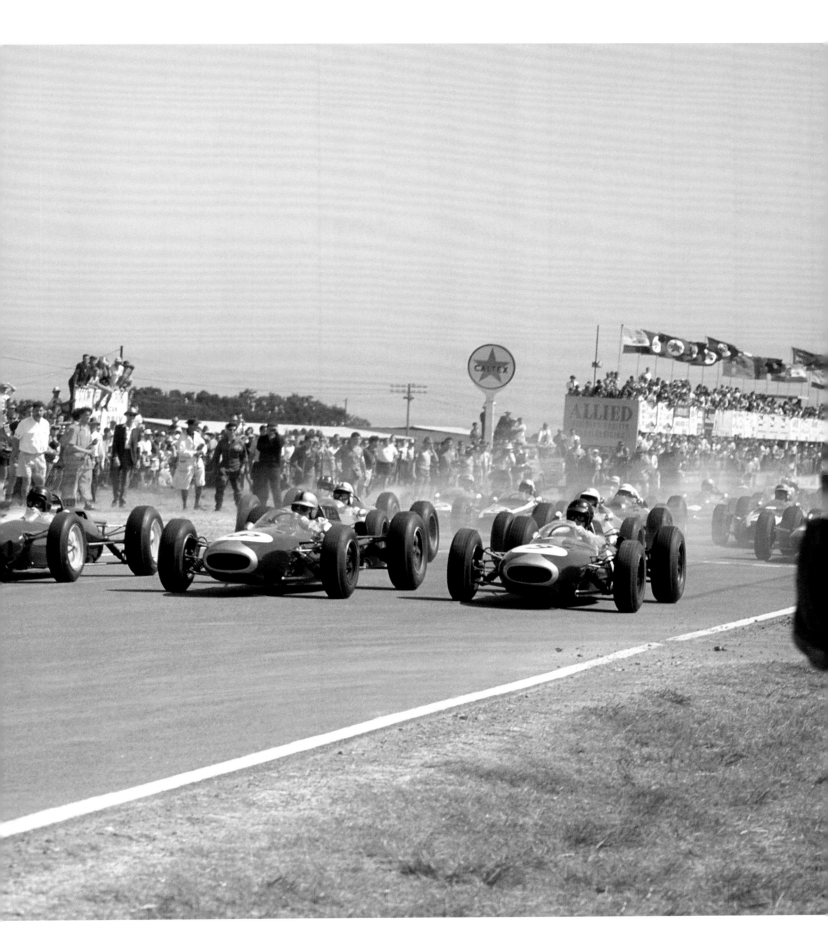

1964

THWARTED AGAIN IN THE SERIES FINALE

The Lotus 25 remained competitive into a third season. Jim, partnered by Peter Arundell until he was injured in a Formula 2 race, and then by Mike Spence, secured three wins from the first five championship races. But the 25 was evolved into the Lotus 33, which was pressed into service before its durability had been proved: Jimmy failed to finish any of the remaining five races. His title defence went all the way to an especially cruel finale in Mexico, where an engine problem ended his hopes. John Surtees won the title for Ferrari, and Jim ended up third. At Indianapolis, Jim broke the track record in putting his Lotus on pole position for the 500-mile race, but its rear suspension collapsed when he was leading. He consoled himself by winning regularly in Formula 2, sports and saloon cars.

RIGHT Jim has the 1964 title in his pocket as he shoots the Peraltada curve in Mexico City, leading the World Championship finale from his fifth pole position of the season. But it was not to be. With 10 laps to go, he noticed a trail of oil as he entered the hairpin, and changed his line. Next time round, he saw a second trail there. And realised it was his oil...

LEFT Jimmy with Colin Chapman after a fortuitous victory in the 'News of the World' Trophy at Goodwood, the only one of four pre-championship Formula 1 races he finished. Jim started his Lotus 25 in the middle of the front row, flanked by Jack Brabham's new Brabham BT11 and Graham Hill's new BRM P261, and was involved from the outset in a battle with these two and Bruce McLaren's Cooper. Brabham departed with a burst tyre, and McLaren in a collision with Innes Ireland's BRP-BRM, leaving Jim, driving with an inoperative clutch, trailing Hill. Two laps from the chequer, the new BRM suffered a total ignition failure.

ABOVE Jim leads the field from pole position on the opening lap of the Grand Prix de Pau street race. The prototype Lotus 32, powered by the new Cosworth SCA engine and operated for Lotus by Ron Harris, is pursued by the superceded, MAE powered Lotus 27 of his team mate, Peter Arundell, and Richard Attwood's Midland Racing Partnership Lola T54. Jim made the first race for the new, 1-litre Formula 2 a bore, winning very easily from Attwood and Arundell.

LEFT Jim passes the railway station during Monaco Grand Prix qualifying, headed for pole position here for the third year running. He led from the start but clipped a strawbale at the chicane on the first lap, possibly breaking the rear anti-roll bar, the mounting of which was later found to be faulty. Nevertheless, he built up a 10sec lead over Dan Gurney's Brabham and Graham Hill's BRM until, under threat of a black flag, Colin Chapman called him into pit-lane on lap 36 to have what remained of the trailing roll bar removed. He rejoined in third place and was swiftly engaged in a three-way battle for the lead. It was resolved when Gurney's gearbox broke and Jim fell back with fading oil pressure. The Climax V8 seized with four laps remaining but Jim was classified fourth behind a second consecutive BRM 1–2 for Hill and Richie Ginther, and Peter Arundell in the other Lotus 25.

ABOVE Jim hurtles a Lotus Cortina down through the Glade at Crystal Palace on his way to an outright victory in the saloon car race there in mid-May, leading Peter Arundell to a 1–2 after Jack Sears's Ford Galaxie had burst a tyre. Frank Gardner and Chris Craft drove two more Lotus Cortinas to beat Gawaine Baillie's Galaxie into fifth place. Jim was unbeaten all season in the 2-litre class of the British Saloon Car Championship and his eight wins, including three overall, secured the 1964 title.

LEFT Sand on Jim's right-side tyres prove that he has been using all the track and a little more in driving his Lotus 25 to a great win in the Dutch Grand Prix. Battle was rejoined at Zandvoort with Brabham's Dan Gurney and BRM's Graham Hill, with Ferrari's John Surtees fourth on the grid. Jim outdragged them to Tarzan and went away at half a second a lap, immaculately controlling the race and winning by 53sec from Surtees, the only man he did not lap. Peter Arundell made it a 1–3 for Team Lotus with Hill fourth, hampered by fuel starvation, and Gurney parked with broken steering.

LEFT Jim with Ford's Dick Bauer at Indianapolis after driving a record-breaking, 158.828mph pole position with the new Lotus 34. Jim would be joined on the front row by Bobby Marshman in Lindsey Hopkins's Lotus 29 (the car crashed during practice here by Dan Gurney the previous May) and Rodger Ward in the new, mid-engined Watson-Ford. Gurney would line up on the outside of the second row with Parnelli Jones and defending USAC champion AJ Foyt in two of the big, front-engined 'roadsters'. Note Bauer's 'Gurney for President' badge – something of which Jim approved. He and Dan were close friends and were similar in terms of their dignity, refinement and love of cars.

BELOW Jim speeds into Turn One at 'The Brickyard' with his Lotus 34, a heavily updated 29 powered by a new, quad-cam, fuel-injected Ford V8. He took the lead at the start of the 500 but the race was stopped after two laps following an appalling, fiery accident, involving seven cars, which killed popular veteran Eddie Sachs and promising rookie Dave MacDonald, and critically injured Ronnie Duman. It took 105 minutes to get the race restarted.

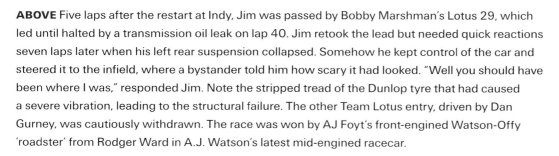

ABOVE Five laps after the restart at Indy, Jim was passed by Bobby Marshman's Lotus 29, which led until halted by a transmission oil leak on lap 40. Jim retook the lead but needed quick reactions seven laps later when his left rear suspension collapsed. Somehow he kept control of the car and steered it to the infield, where a bystander told him how scary it had looked. "Well you should have been where I was," responded Jim. Note the stripped tread of the Dunlop tyre that had caused a severe vibration, leading to the structural failure. The other Team Lotus entry, driven by Dan Gurney, was cautiously withdrawn. The race was won by AJ Foyt's front-engined Watson-Offy 'roadster' from Rodger Ward in A.J. Watson's latest mid-engined racecar.

RIGHT This famous photograph shows Jim chatting after the Belgian Grand Prix with Dan Gurney – his team mate at Indy a fortnight before, but now an arch-rival again in Formula 1. Gurney had this race wrapped up, leading by 40sec and surely about to achieve Brabham's first victory, when he ran short of fuel with three laps to go. He pitted for a top-up, but there was no fuel in his pit, so he carried on. Graham Hill moved into the lead for BRM – and ran out of fuel on the last lap. Bruce McLaren took over for Cooper – and ran out of fuel as he approached La Source. Along came Jim, who had rejoined after dropping out of third place to top up with water in the Team Lotus pit. He passed the helpless McLaren 100 yards before the line – and ran out of fuel on his slowdown lap. He parked up at Stavelot next to Gurney, whose fuel tank was also dry, and they swapped their race stories for a while until they heard a public address announcement that Jim had won. He had no idea...

ABOVE Jim reaches the foot of the hill at Rouen-les-Essarts as he puts the prototype Lotus 33 on pole position for the French Grand Prix, beating Graham Hill's two-year-old lap record by about 7sec. He and Dan Gurney dominated the race and Jim led for 30 laps until catching sight of oil smoke in his mirrors, and diving into the pits: holed piston. Gurney went on finally to score Brabham's maiden victory in a World Championship race. Jim left Rouen still leading the championship with 21 points, but Hill's second place brought him to 20. John Surtees's non-finish here left him on six...

RIGHT Jim in pole position on the grid for the first British Grand Prix to be held at Brands Hatch, which was seen by 100,000 people. The week before, Peter Arundell had been badly injured in the Formula 2 race at Reims, and Jim was partnered here by Mike Spence. He led the race all the way, harried at first by Dan Gurney's Brabham until its transistor box caught fire, then by Graham Hill's BRM, which maintained a determined pursuit to the very end. Jim's third straight victory in this event was hard-earned. John Surtees's V8 Ferrari finished a distant third. The RAC's Dean Delamont offers last-minute advice.

RIGHT Atrocious weather on the seven-mile Solitude circuit near Stuttgart, the week after Brands, caused a 40-minute delay before this popular non-championship race was started in unremitting rain. Jim was on pole with the Lotus 33, lost the lead to John Surtees's Ferrari 158, but took it back as the rain eased to win by 10sec. Graham Hill qualified third but his BRM slithered off the track and into a telegraph pole.

ABOVE The Zeltweg airfield circuit was the venue of the first Austrian Grand Prix, and the concrete surfaces did for all the championship contenders. They dominated qualifying but all departed the race, Graham Hill's BRM with a busted distributor drive, John Surtees's Ferrari 158 with a rear suspension failure, Jim's Lotus with a broken driveshaft, and Dan Gurney's Brabham with a front suspension breakage. Lorenzo Bandini won with his V6 Ferrari.

LEFT The day after a non-finish in the German Grand Prix, which was ominously won by John Surtees for Ferrari, Jim exits the Druids hairpin at Brands Hatch, driving his Ron Harris Team Lotus 32 to an impressive victory in the British Eagle Trophy Formula 2 race during the big August international meeting. He beat a string of five Brabhams including the works team cars of Jack Brabham and Denny Hulme and Graham Hill's John Coombs entry, which had pipped the Lotus to pole position.

LEFT This photograph tells us everything we want to know about the handling of the Lotus 30 sports-racing car, not to mention Jim's commitment. This car, built in response to American demand for V8 'big-bangers', was based on a narrow 'backbone' chassis that was nowhere near stiff enough to handle the 350bhp output of its 4.7-litre Ford V8. Somehow Jim put the beast on the front row of the grid for the Tourist Trophy at Goodwood, second fastest behind Bruce McLaren's Cooper-Oldsmobile (a converted Formula 1 chassis) and almost 1sec quicker than Graham Hill's Ferrari 330P. Jim even led McLaren for a while and can be seen here in the classic combination that would see him through to the end of 1965 – Bell Magnum helmet, light blue Dunlop two-piece overalls and Jim Clark (kangaroo skin) driving gloves.

LEFT Lap 80 of the 130-lap Tourist Trophy, and Jim has the Lotus 30 in the Goodwood pit-lane for fuel and oil. Among the group looking down from the pit counter is Bruce McLaren, who had abandoned the fray when his race-leading Cooper-Oldsmobile broke its clutch. Jim had taken over at the front and was leading by more than a lap when he made this pitstop. But the Ford V8 would not immediately restart and, later, an unscheduled stop for a suspension repair put him completely out of contention. The race was won by Graham Hill's 4-litre Ferrari.

ABOVE Jim with Mike Spence and Colin Chapman in the pit-lane of the Autodromo Nazionale di Monza, having found no answer to the pace of the V8 Ferrari 158. John Surtees's victory on the Nürburgring had proved that the Scuderia's act was finally coming together. Despite having been concussed in crashing his Ferrari sportscar the week before at Goodwood, 'Big John' was on pole here, almost 1sec clear of Dan Gurney's Brabham and Graham Hill's BRM, and almost 2sec ahead of Jim in fourth position on the grid, reverting to a Lotus 25 for this race. Hill's clutch seized on the line and Jim mixed it with Gurney and Surtees until a piston broke. Gurney's engine also failed and Surtees won easily. Now the points table showed Hill leading from Jim and Surtees, 32–30–28.

ABOVE The United States Grand Prix, lap 14: Jim has just taken the lead from John Surtees's Ferrari 158, which is racing at Watkins Glen in the white-and-blue colours of Luigi Chinetti's NART team. Jim had bagged pole position, then lost out at the start, but his recovery was for nothing. His fuel pump packed up after 43 laps. He took over Mike Spence's Lotus 33 and drove it to seventh place. Graham Hill's BRM won the race, with Surtees second, setting up an exciting title-decider in Mexico City three weeks later.

RIGHT The title contenders went to the finale in Mexico City with Graham Hill leading John Surtees and Jim in the points table, 39–34–30, and Ferrari leading BRM and Lotus in the Constructors' Championship, 43–42–36. Jimmy had to win the race to complete a successful defence of the Drivers' Championship, with Surtees no higher than third, and Hill unplaced. From the pole, he was leading comfortably when Hill, running third far behind Dan Gurney's Brabham, was punted into a guardrail by Lorenzo Bandini's Ferrari, bending the BRM's exhaust cluster. Hill needed two pitstops to fix the problem – and Surtees had been promoted only to fourth. Jim had the title in his pocket. He eased up, and everyone thought he was cruising. In fact, his Climax V8 had sprung an oil leak. As he started his very last lap, it died. Gurney drove past the stricken Lotus to win the race, and Bandini waved his team leader through to second place. And both championships went to Maranello.

1 9 6 5

A SECOND F1 TITLE – AND THE INDY 500

This momentous year, Jim Clark achieved the most success by any driver in the history of international motor racing. He gave notice of the potential for the season by landing 10 wins from 15 starts (including heats) during the Tasman Series in Australasia. In Formula 1, his six victories from the first seven Grands Prix, four of them from pole and all from the front row, wrapped up his second World Championship on the first day of August – which was just as well, because engine failures stopped his Lotus 33 in all three remaining races. He did not contest the Monaco Grand Prix because it clashed with the Indianapolis 500, which he won at his third attempt. Including Formula 2, sports and saloon car events, Jimmy secured a grand total of 32 victories (among 40 podiums) from 61 starts.

RIGHT On New Year's Day, Jim starts the season with a perfect South African Grand Prix victory with the upgraded Lotus 33. From pole position, with a second to spare over defending champion John Surtees (Ferrari 158) and Jack Brabham (Brabham BT11), he led all the way. Leading Surtees by half a minute with five laps remaining, as it began to drizzle, he kept himself alert by driving the first 100mph lap on the 2.4-mile East London circuit.

LEFT Back from the Tasman Series in mid-March, Jim won one of the heats of the Formula 1 Race of Champions at Brands Hatch (then crashing heavily in the second heat), the Guards Trophy sportscar event at Silverstone with the fearsome Lotus 30, and a three-hour race at Sebring, Florida, with a Lotus Cortina. Then he conquered the Formula 1 Ferraris again, this time on their home ground here at Syracuse, where John Surtees finished second in the V8 car and Lorenzo Bandini third in the new flat-12. It was Jim's 15th victory (and 16th pole) from 23 starts so far in 1965. This was already promising...

ABOVE From South Africa, Team Lotus went to Australasia, where Jim contested the Tasman Series for the first time at the wheel of a Lotus 32B. Three victories in as many weeks in January in New Zealand, at Levin, Christchurch and Teretonga (pictured), all but secured the title, but Jim made sure with another win at Warwick Farm, in Australia, despite the loss of third gear early in the race. He won the championship with 11 points over Bruce McLaren (Cooper) and 14 over Jack Brabham.

RIGHT Jim with Colin Chapman after his victory in the 'Sunday Mirror' Trophy at Goodwood. This April day, in stormy conditions in Sussex, Jimmy defeated Graham Hill and Jack Brabham in the Formula 1 race, Jack Sears and Roy Pierpoint in the saloon car race, and Bruce McLaren and David Hobbs in the sportscar race. It is a Team Lotus year, and they already know it. Behind them is the BARC's secretary of the meeting, Grahame White.

BELOW Jim continued to entertain British fans in 1965 in saloon car racing, leading the fight for Ford and Lotus against the American muscle-cars. A measure of his enduring charisma is that one of his 1965 Lotus Cortinas, a car also raced by Jack Sears and John Whitmore, changed hands for almost £137,000 at auction in December 2007.

RIGHT Jim winning on a wet track with the Lotus 32 to reach a hat-trick of Formula 2 victories on the tricky street circuit in Pau, where this time he lapped the entire field. The abandoned car is Denny Hulme's crashed Brabham BT16. Jim went on to secure further 1965 Formula 2 victories for Ron Harris Team Lotus, at Crystal Palace, Rouen, Brands Hatch and Albi. Hulme, Jack Brabham, Graham Hill, Jochen Rindt and Alan Rees were successful in Brabhams, and John Surtees, Richard Attwood and Chris Amon in Lolas, but none of these won more than once. Jim ended the season with the British and French Championship titles to his increasingly valuable name.

ABOVE The Lotus 38 was a full monocoque, designed for Colin Chapman by Len Terry to incorporate USAC's new fuel cell regulations, which had been introduced as a consequence of the awful fires the year before. It was powered by a new version of the quad-cam Ford V8, delivering 500bhp on methanol to a two-speed ZF transmission. Here is Jim undertaking the obligatory Indy photo-call.

RIGHT Jim and Colin Chapman in the pit-lane at the Indianapolis Motor Speedway during their third attempt to win the historic 500-mile race. It was more difficult now, because the American teams had got the message, and 27 of the 33 cars that qualified were mid-engined. Dan Gurney had moved on, having formed his All-American Racers team, and was replaced as Jim's team mate for this race by another American, Bobby Johns. Jim received several new pairs of overalls at Indy, culminating in the locally made Hinchmans he wore in '67 and '68. Because of that US style, he was amongst the first F1 drivers to race with his name embroidered on his overalls. He stopped short of including his blood group, however.

LEFT Looking more than a little strained, Jimmy confers with Colin Chapman after a practice run in his Lotus 38, as a Goodyear engineer checks the tyre temperatures. Clark won the race on Firestones, but in those days it was common practice to try the opposition's tyres whenever possible. Ultimately the new car proved the class of the field in Jim's hands and obliterated the track record in qualifying – but then the very determined AJ Foyt went out with Sheraton Thompson's older Lotus 34 and pipped Jim to pole position. Dan Gurney, in AAR's new Lotus 38, completed the front row for the rolling start.

ABOVE Jim heads for his famous victory in the Indy 500. He led the first lap, trailed AJ Foyt on the second, then repassed him and hauled the Lotus 38 into the distance. Aided by slick pitwork, provided by the legendary Woods Brothers stock car racing crew who had been specially hired by Colin Chapman, and by much better tyre wear (courtesy of Jim Clark!), Jim was leading Foyt by about a minute when the pole man was halted on lap 115 by a transmission failure. Jim eased up towards the end but still won by very nearly two minutes. Parnelli Jones in J.C. Agajanian's Lotus-Ford, Indy rookie Mario Andretti in Al Dean's Brawner-Ford, Al Miller in Jerry Alderman's Lotus-Ford and Gordon Johncock in a front-engined Offy 'roadster' were the only others to complete the 200-lap distance. Team mate Bobby Johns finished seventh.

ABOVE With his name finally on the Borg-Warner Trophy, Jim seems bemused by the media attention after his magnificent Indianapolis victory, the first achieved at an average speed exceeding 150mph. It paid US$150,000 in prize money, then the biggest ever in racing history. The day before, Graham Hill had won his third straight Monaco Grand Prix – and less than $2000.

RIGHT The weekend after Indy, Jim won both heats and the final of a Formula 2 event at Crystal Palace before resuming his Formula 1 programme in the Belgian Grand Prix. He was outqualified by Graham Hill, but the BRM's lead only endured as far as the Malmedy corner, and thereafter the Lotus 33 was gone. In wet conditions yet again at Spa-Francorchamps, Hill faded to fifth place and Jim's 45sec victory margin was over Jackie Stewart in the other BRM P261, restoring the lead of the World Championship he had established in South Africa.

LEFT The start of the French Grand Prix on the tight Clermont-Ferrand circuit, where Jim put together another of his perfect performances, with pole position, a record fastest lap, and a flag-to-flag victory. He was leading by 3sec after the first lap and his rivals, led here by Lorenzo Bandini with the flat-12 Ferrari and Jackie Stewart with a V8 BRM, were given no chance whatsoever. Jim led every lap of every race the 33 finished. Following a cheery (and impromptu) meeting with the Russian cosmonaut Yuri Gagarin, at the Clermont airport the previous Wednesday, Colin Chapman managed to tip his Peugeot hire car into a ditch while attempting to find an elusive hotel late at night. Two of this three passengers – Jim and Mike Spence – were basically uninjured, but Sally Stokes cut her head on the windscreen. Jim promptly fainted at the sight of her blood and had to be nursed back into reality by the extremely together Sally!

RIGHT Jim scampers along the start-finish straight at Silverstone, leading the British Grand Prix from the pole. Installed in the outstanding Lotus 33 chassis, the four-valve version of the Coventry Climax V8 enabled him to pursue his policy of building up leads as big as possible in case of any problems late in the races. With 15 laps to go here, he had established 35sec over Graham Hill when he saw his oil pressure fading. He set out to nurse his car all the way to the finish, and did it to perfection. With four laps left, the pressure gauge zeroed. But the BRM was held at bay by 3.2sec.

ABOVE Jim and the Team Lotus crew prepare for the victory parade after his nerve-wracking victory at Silverstone. Team mate Mike Spence (at left), who has finished fourth, is along for the ride, and so is Sally Stokes, Jim's girlfriend.

RIGHT Jim, who was under 5ft 8in tall, stands on a rear wheel of his Lotus 33 during qualifying for the Dutch Grand Prix to get a better view of his rivals as they speed past the pits on their way to the Tarzan hairpin. He always could keep himself alone with his thoughts among throngs of people.

ABOVE Jim's soft heart was visible to all whenever animals were about. This police horse was at Zandvoort to help control a 60,000 race day crowd. Before the start, Team Lotus principal Colin Chapman was involved in a scuffle with a policeman who was trying to manhandle him off the dummy grid. When it was over, Chapman was arrested, and held until the matter was sorted out with an apology.

RIGHT Jim is the centre of media attention at Zandvoort. This time it took him five laps to get into the lead of the Dutch Grand Prix. Richie Ginther led the first two laps with the Honda V12, and Graham Hill the next three for BRM. Then Jim was gone again...

It is 1 August 1965: when this day is over, Jim will be the new World Champion. Here he glances across at the backmarkers as he again outdrives the opposition at the Nürburgring. His absolute superiority had been amply demonstrated by a scintillating pole position. On race day, he broke the lap record on the first lap – from a standing start. In fact, his winning average was faster than the old lap record, and his fastest lap was the first driven at more than 100mph during any race here.

LEFT Having won at Silverstone and Goodwood with the difficult Lotus 30, Jim was equipped with the latest Lotus 40 sports-racing car for the Guards Trophy race at Brands Hatch, where he defeated the Brabhams to win the Formula 2 race. Richie Ginther famously called this 5.7-litre V8, 500bhp car: "The Lotus 30 with 10 more mistakes." Jim would have agreed, because this was just embarrassing. He spun twice during the first heat in trying to keep up with the Lolas and McLaren-Elvas, eventually finishing 10th. Mercifully the transmission seized in the second heat. At the end of the season, somehow, he raced a Lotus 40 to second place in the big Times Grand Prix sportscar race at Riverside, California, behind Hap Sharp's Chaparral 2.

ABOVE Three Grands Prix remained after Jim had clinched his second championship. He started on pole position at Monza but dropped out of a classic slipstream battle with a broken fuel pump. He was second on the grid at Watkins Glen but succumbed to an engine failure after only 11 laps. And he was on pole again for the finale here in Mexico City, but lasted only eight laps before the Climax V8 let him down again. The car following is Rob Walker's Brabham, driven by Jo Bonnier. BRM had triumphed in the Italian and United States Grands Prix, but this race, the last of the 1.5-litre era, was won by Richie Ginther's Honda.

1 9 6 6

A SINGLE SUCCESS
WITH THE BRM H16

Far from mounting any defence of his Formula 1 title, Jim had to endure his worst season as a Team Lotus driver. Few teams were ready for the new, 3-litre formula, although Brabham had a deal with Repco for an Oldsmobile-based V8, while Cooper had sourced a modified Maserati sportscar V12. Jim started out with the old Lotus 33, fitted with a 2-litre Coventry Climax V8, while BRM built its complex new H16 engine for its own team and the new Lotus 43. The new car was not deemed race-ready for Jim until Monza in September. By then, the title defence was lost to Jack Brabham, but Jim produced a tremendous, wholly unexpected victory at Watkins Glen, elevating himself to sixth in the World Championship. Lotus also let him down with its new Formula 2 car and there were no victories from nine attempts.

RIGHT Jimmy dives through Cascades with the 3-litre, H16 BRM-engined Lotus 43, during the 1966 Oulton Park Gold Cup. The factory BRM team couldn't tame their own, massively complicated beast, but Jim was able to massage it to an amazing victory in the US Grand Prix a few weeks after this photograph was taken.

LEFT Jim did the 1966 Tasman Series with Team Lotus but was unlucky, unable to duplicate his domination of the previous season, especially in the face of powerful opposition from BRM with Graham Hill and Jackie Stewart. His only victories with the Climax-powered Lotus 39 came in a dead-heat with Stewart in a qualifying race at Invercargill and here at Warwick Farm, the first of the Australian venues, where Jim gives the thumbs-up to his good mate, Charles Brittlebank. Jim had three second places from the 10 races, but also three DNFs. Stewart won the title, with Hill second and Jim third. Jim loved the Tasman Series, and particularly his time in Sydney, where he learned to fly with Jim Hazleton at Bankstown. Every February from '66 to '68 he flew daily from Bankstown and/or Orange, where there was less activity and thus earlier slot times. Jim also became close friends with Geoffrey Sykes, the Warwick Farm promoter who began life with the BARC at Goodwood. Jim loved Geoff's grass-and-picket fence atmosphere at what was, at the time, the world's safest motor racing circuit.

ABOVE On his return to Europe from the Tasman Series, Jim's first track action came on Good Friday at Oulton Park, where he landed pole positions with a Formula 2 Lotus 35 and a Lotus Cortina. But the meeting was snowed off, so his first European race was here at Snetterton on Easter Monday. The new Group 5 regulations allowed more performance from the Cortina and Jim is pictured in an outrageous slide, leading Jack Brabham (Mustang) and Peter Arundell in the other Cortina. However, 185bhp was not enough to beat the American V8s here and Jim was monstered into third place by Brabham and Brian Muir (Ford Galaxie).

ABOVE Jim shares a light moment at Monaco with Jackie Stewart and Graham Hill, his BRM rivals, before the opening race of the 3-litre Formula 1. All were equipped here with 2-litre versions of their V8 engines from 1965. Jim took pole position yet again on this circuit, while the BRMs shared the second row behind John Surtees's 3-litre V12 Ferrari, which was out inside 15 laps. For 1966, Jim switched to white Les Leston fire-resistant overalls and also the latest Les Leston helmet.

RIGHT Jim has his Lotus 33 on full lock as he negotiates the Station hairpin in Monte Carlo. The Monaco jinx remained: at the start, his gearbox jammed itself in fourth, and he arrived at Ste Devote in last place. It took him 63 laps to do the impossible. He caught up with the race-leading BRMs – and immediately his rear suspension collapsed, sending him skittering into retirement at the Gasometer hairpin (again!). Jackie Stewart won, with Graham Hill third behind Lorenzo Bandini's 2.4-litre V6 Ferrari.

LEFT Jim in the pit-lane at the Brickyard with the 1966 version of the USAC Lotus 38. This year, Ford switched its backing to Dan Gurney's AAR team, but Colin Chapman put together a sponsorship deal with Andy Granatelli's STP fuel additive brand. The team called that colour 'Granatelli Green' and, after the race, Jim was sure STP stood for 'Spinning Takes Practice'. His team mate in the Indy 500 was Al Unser.

LEFT A moment for reflection in the Indianapolis pit-lane, showing some of the strain of transatlantic Indy racing in the midst of an F1 season. Jimmy was preoccupied with the difficult handling of the latest Lotus-Ford throughout the month of May, but he returned to the Brickyard from Monaco and qualified his car in the centre of the front row between Mario Andretti in Al Dean's Brabham-based Brawner-Ford and George Snider in a Coyote-Ford.

ABOVE Jim storms the start/finish straight at Indianapolis in pursuit of the race leader, Lloyd Ruby in one of AAR's Eagles. This race had to be suspended for 84 minutes after a startline collision triggered an unprecedented pile-up that eliminated 16 cars, including AJ Foyt's Coyote and Dan Gurney's Eagle. Jim inherited the lead when Mario Andretti's Brawner was stopped by a broken engine, but lost it to Ruby by spinning when headed for a scheduled pitstop on lap 62. Back in the lead on lap 85, he spun again, resuming in what he thought was third place behind Ruby and Jackie Stewart (Lola). When both retired, Jimmy believed he had won, so he drove to Victory Lane. Graham Hill's American Red Ball Lola was already there. Team Lotus had not noticed Hill passing Jim in the confusion of the second spin.

ABOVE Jim shows the photographer the neat lines of his Lotus 33 as he exits Stirling's Bend at Brands Hatch during the British Grand Prix. Fifth in qualifying, he could not match the pace of the 3-litre Brabham-Repcos and Dan Gurney's 2.7 Eagle-Climax. On race day, his American friend went out early, and Jim spent this afternoon chasing down Graham Hill's BRM for third place, a lap behind Jack Brabham and Denny Hulme. The bid fell tantalisingly short.

RIGHT A sensational performance by Jim might have delivered a victory in the Dutch Grand Prix, but overheating caused this pitstop with 14 of the 90 laps remaining. Jim qualified his 2-litre Lotus-Climax in third place, beaten only by the Brabham-Repcos, and engaged them both from the start. After Denny Hulme's BT20 went out with a faulty ignition system, Jim passed Jack Brabham for the lead, and he was still in front when a water leak intervened. Eight laps after his first stop, Jim had to top up with yet more water, and wound up third behind Brabham and BRM's Graham Hill. Dick Scammell (right), who would later run Cosworth Engineering, and Leo Wybrott, who now lives in Australia, look suitably concerned at the back of the car.

LAPS TO BE COMPLETED

SHELL

200

PHK 615D

215

LEFT Jim opened the August international meeting at Brands Hatch by winning the saloon car race at a canter from Jack Oliver in a Ford Mustang, Peter Arundell in the other works Lotus Cortina and Brian Muir in a Ford Galaxie. Apart from a couple of successes in the Tasman Series at the start of the year, and the triumph in the US Grand Prix, Jim's only race wins in the whole of 1966 came in Lotus Cortinas. And there were only two of those...

ABOVE Jimmy would try anything once, and he had a one-off run in the four-wheel-drive Felday 4 sports-racing car at the Brands Hatch August International. The car, powered by a BRM V8, was undergeared, but he qualified it 10th overall, comfortably fastest in the 2-litre class. Jim finished eighth in the first of two races making up the Guards Trophy event, winning the class, but was black-flagged out of the second race when the engine started leaking oil. John Surtees's Lola won on aggregate for Lola, from Chris Amon's McLaren, while Max Wilson's Brabham BT8 inherited the 2-litre win. *(Photo courtesy of The Klemantaski Collection)*

LEFT Jim smokes the rear tyres of the Lotus 43 BRM on the starting grid at Watkins Glen. He had first raced the 43 at Monza, where he had qualified on the front row and raced in fifth place until stopped by a transmission failure. The 43-BRM package may have had insufficient development, but the 16-cylinder engine had plenty of power and Jim was outqualified for the United States Grand Prix only by Jack Brabham's championship-winning Brabham BT20. Then the H16 broke a valve. BRM's H16 engined P83 cars safely qualified fifth and sixth and the team had a spare engine, which was loaned to Lotus and fitted to Clark's car overnight.

ABOVE Jim acknowledges the extrovert Tex Hopkins and the chequered flag at Watkins Glen after leading the final 53 laps of the United States Grand Prix, although no one had expected his Lotus 43 to last the distance. Jack Brabham, Lorenzo Bandini in the solo Ferrari 312 and John Surtees in a works Cooper-Maserati led the early action, with Jim fourth. Surtees was tripped up when lapping Peter Arundell's Lotus-BRM V8, Bandini's V12 broke, and then so did Brabham's Repco V8. Alas for Jimmy, this performance would not be repeated in the Mexico City finale: an engine failure during practice dowsed Jim with hot water and oil, and on race day the gear linkage broke.

ABOVE Jim had an offer from Ford to do the RAC Rally in one of four works Lotus Cortinas, and the experienced Brian Melia was offered as his co-driver. In October, Melia drove to Snetterton, where Jim was testing the 1967 USAC Lotus, to persuade him to accept the drive, and he did so after testing one of the cars on Ford's test track at Boreham. On the event itself, Jim startled the professional rally community by setting consistently quick times on the forest tracks. When he was not among the fastest five, it was usually because of frustratingly frequent punctures, and he actually 'won' three special stages.

RIGHT Jim had his Lotus Cortina in sixth position at Aviemore at the end of the second day of the RAC Rally, but ruined his very real chance of victory early on the last day by sidewiping a projecting rock on the 45th of the 63 stages (ironically, the first in Scotland). It was 45 minutes before Jim and navigator Brian Melia could resume and, five stages later, the damaged car slid into a ditch and rolled. It was the last time the British public saw Jim in action with anything but a Formula 1 car. One of his works team mates, Bengt Soderstrom, won the event with Gunnar Palm. Jim's Christmas card that year showed a picture of the dented rally Cortina with the caption; "Car by Ford and Lotus; coachwork by Clark."

1 9 6 7

A WINNER AGAIN
IN THE LOTUS 49

At the end of 1966, hounded by the Inland Revenue, Jim left Scotland and set up home in Bermuda. The arrangement with the authorities was that, for three years, he could have only a minimal presence in Britain. Consequently he raced only once in his native country during 1967, when he won the British Grand Prix at Silverstone. However, his professional fortunes took a dramatic turn for the better after his woeful 1966 season. Having won the Tasman title again, Jim was partnered by Graham Hill in what was effectively Ford's works team, equipped with the Lotus 49 and the new, Ford-financed Cosworth DFV engine. Jim famously won first time out with the DFV at Zandvoort. He won again at Silverstone, Watkins Glen and Mexico City, but the speed of the new car was not matched by its reliability.

RIGHT Formula 1 changed fundamentally early in June 1967, when the new Ford Cosworth DFV engine appeared at Zandvoort in the purpose-built Lotus 49. Here Jim leads Pedro Rodriguez's Cooper-Maserati, Jackie Stewart's BRM, Denny Hulme's Brabham and Mike Parkes's Ferrari into the Hunzerug left-hander early in the Dutch Grand Prix, setting off for an emphatic victory that seemed to put him firmly on course for a third World Championship.

LEFT The 1967 World Championship began on 2 January at Kyalami, where Jim put the Lotus 43 BRM third on the grid behind the Brabham-Repcos, and then found the H16 engine hunting for fuel immediately after the start of the South African Grand Prix. He ran in the top six for about 20 laps but the fuel pump was obviously on its last legs and, when sticking throttle slides made life in the cockpit even less comfortable, he called it a day. In a race of high attrition, both Jack Brabham and Denny Hulme were delayed, and Pedro Rodriguez, being given a trial outing in a works Cooper-Maserati, came along to win.

ABOVE Jim was equipped with the faithful, 2-litre Climax V8 powered Lotus 33 for the Tasman Series that occupied him in January and February. This year Team Lotus sent only one car down-under, with two engines and two Kiwi mechanics, whereas BRM mounted a substantially bigger effort in defence of Jackie Stewart's title, and Brabham also raced two 2.5-litre Repco V8 cars. As in 1965, however, Jim was too strong. He won in New Zealand at Christchurch (adding non-championship wins at Levin and Teretonga), and then in Australia at Lakeside and Sandown Park. He was beaten into second place twice by Stewart (chasing him here at Levin) and once by Jack Brabham, and claimed the title for a second time with 45 points to his rivals' 18 apiece.

ABOVE Back in Europe from his successful sojourn down-under, Jim contested three races for the new, 1.6-litre Formula 2 during April, and put the new Lotus 48 on pole position for all three. At Pau, he was delayed in the race by two pitstops but finished fourth, defeated by the new Brabhams of Jochen Rindt, Denny Hulme and Alan Rees. He turned the tables on them with a great win on the super-quick Montjuich Park circuit in Barcelona, where he is pictured leading Jack Brabham, Rindt and Hulme, but a broken gearbox ended his run on an icy Nürburgring South Circuit, where Rindt won again. Later in the season, Jim landed two more victories, at Jarama and Keimola, but the 48 was difficult and fragile and this was Rindt's year.

RIGHT The heavy, USAC-derived Lotus 43 H16 would have been hopeless in the tight confines of Monte Carlo, so Team Lotus reverted to the more nimble 33 for the race in early May. Both its cars were equipped with 2-litre V8s, Jim's with a Climax and Graham Hill's with a BRM. Jim, pictured leading Pedro Rodriguez's Cooper down the slope from the Mirabeau hotel, qualified a brilliant fifth, behind four 3-litre cars, but found himself squeezed into the escape road at the chicane on the second lap. He recovered magnificently and, aided by attrition, was up in fourth place when a broken suspension damper put him in the wall at Tabac. He was long gone when Lorenzo Bandini's Ferrari, chasing leader Denny Hulme's Brabham, had the appalling accident for which this race is remembered. This was Jim's last Monaco: there had been four pole positions here, but never a win.

ABOVE The Indianapolis 500 was now exclusively contested by mid-engined cars and Team Lotus was now just a regular customer with regard to its 4.2-litre Ford V8 engines. Jim hated Indy in '67. The BRM engines never materialised, obliging Lotus to field obsolete cars at the last minute. In previous years it had only been the potential for success that had made the 'ballyhoo' tolerable. Jim and Graham Hill, previous winners and now team mates, qualified 16th and 31st respectively. They were running inconspicuously in the midfield when the race was suspended due to rain and, shortly after the restart the next day, Hill's one-off Lotus 42F went out with a burned piston, and Jim's old Lotus 38 with oiled plugs. This 500 was famously led until three laps from the end by Parnelli Jones in STP's turbine powered car. A gearbox bearing failure handed the win to AJ Foyt's Coyote-Ford. *(Photo courtesy of Bob Tronolone)*

RIGHT Jim at Zandvoort with Keith Duckworth, the creator of the Ford Cosworth DFV. Duckworth's new engine changed Formula 1 completely, making available an inexpensive 3-litre V8 that allowed the small, British-based constructors to thrive. That process would start in 1968: for the rest of this season, Team Lotus held an exclusive deal for this innovative, loadbearing engine. The mechanical frailties of the early Lotus 49 chassis prevented the team from making the most of its substantial power advantage.

ABOVE A broken wheel hub hampered Jim's qualifying effort at Zandvoort with the new Lotus 49 and he could do no better than eighth on the grid, with a lap-time much slower than the one that earned Graham Hill pole position with the sister car. The loadbearing capability of the powerful new Cosworth V8 signalled the beginning of the chassis-engine 'packaging' that has characterised Formula 1 cars ever since.

RIGHT Jim's joyful demeanour after winning in Holland reveals his confidence that the new season will eradicate 1966 from memory. Many other Formula 1 cars had won on début, but none with as little track-test development as the Lotus 49. Graham Hill's lead from pole position at Zandvoort only endured 11 laps before his DFV's timing gear broke. By that early stage, Jim was already up to third. He hunted down the new leader, Jack Brabham, rocketed past him on lap 16 and led for the duration, although a 30sec lead was cut back to 23sec after the new car's brakes played up. Now a tax exile, Jim invited his sisters to Zandvoort to watch his race. It was their first sight of James Clark Jnr (as he was known in the early days in Scotland) in an F1 car and they duly celebrated at the Bouwes Palace Hotel after the race.

RIGHT Jim negotiates the La Source hairpin at Spa-Francorchamps, having secured his first pole with the Lotus 49. He was half a minute in the lead of the Belgian Grand Prix when he lost time in the pits in replacing a broken spark plug. He wound up sixth in the only Grand Prix won by Dan Gurney's Eagle-Weslake V12.

FOLLOWING PAGE The French Grand Prix was run at Le Mans for the first (and to date only) time since 1921, using the permanent Bugatti circuit. Team Lotus was delayed in the French customs and then Jim had a misfire during qualifying, although he has managed to retrieve fourth on the grid. As the flag falls, team mate Graham Hill, on pole position (nearest the pits), Jack Brabham (Brabham-Repco V8) and Dan Gurney (Eagle-Weslake V12) are all smoking their tyres in unison. Alongside Jim on the second row of the grid is Bruce McLaren in the other Eagle, and behind are Denny Hulme (Brabham), a fast-starting Chris Amon (Ferrari V12) and Jochen Rindt (Cooper-Maserati V12), then Chris Irwin and Jackie Stewart in BRMs, and Jo Siffert (Cooper), Mike Spence (BRM) and Pedro Rodriguez (Cooper). The Lotus drivers had a 1–2 going inside six laps, but both cars were parked soon afterwards with identical transmission (CWP) failures. Brabham and Hulme contrived a Brabham 1–2 in their stead.

ABOVE Jim hugging the wall at Silverstone during the British Grand Prix, the only race he contested in Britain all season. He had an almost perfect weekend, qualifying on the pole 0.7sec clear of his team mate, Graham Hill, who then crashed trying to improve. In the race, Hill passed him to take the lead just before half-distance, only to lose time in the pits when a suspension bolt sheared. Jim won at an average speed faster than the Formula 1 lap record, with Denny Hulme's Brabham almost 13sec behind.

RIGHT Jim gets the Lotus 49 droopily airborne at the Flugplatz on the Nürburgring, where he demoralised the opposition with a pole position lap 9.4sec faster than Brabham's Denny Hulme, his closest challenger. He was leading the German Grand Prix when his front suspension collapsed. Hulme won. Note how far Jimmy has been thrown upwards out of the cockpit!

ABOVE Jim, ice cream in hand, enjoys a practice lull at Monza with Kate Eccles, to whom he was close in 1967. To Jim's left sits his close friend and Parisian flat-mate 'Jabby' Crombac. Although now based in Bermuda for tax reasons, Jim spent much of his summer commuting to the races from Paris in a yellow Lotus Elan S3 – a car he told Crombac that allowed him to "rediscover his love of driving".

LEFT Jim during one of the most astonishing drives of his career, at the Italian GP, after a chaotic start that nullified his pole. He was engaged at the front of the race in a classic Monza slipstreaming group, with Graham Hill, Denny Hulme and Jack Brabham, when lap 13 was unlucky: a puncture. He dived into the pits and rejoined 100 yards behind the leading bunch, a lap down. Jim unlapped himself five laps later – and broke the tow in doing so. Now he repeatedly pulverised the lap record (equalling his pole position time), lapping as much as 2sec faster than the leaders. He finally caught them on lap 58, with 10 to go. Then Hill's engine blew. Jim passed John Surtees's Honda and, on lap 61, took the lead from Brabham. These three were fighting it out when Jim, still leading, ran out of fuel on the back straight on the last lap. The Honda won in a photo-finish with Brabham. Jim coasted into third place.

Jim, desperately disappointed, is congratulated by French journalist Bernard Cahier after his incredible drive at Monza. It turned out later that his Lotus 49 still had three gallons of fuel in its tank. Before the start, foam inserts had been put in the cell to prevent surge, and had prevented the pump from picking up the last of the fuel.

LEFT The start of the US Grand Prix at Watkins Glen, and pole man Graham Hill has the lead, chased down the slope by Dan Gurney (Eagle), Jim in the other Lotus 49, Chris Amon (Ferrari V12), defending champion Jack Brabham and Denny Hulme in their Brabhams, Bruce McLaren in the red McLaren, Jackie Stewart (BRM), Jochen Rindt (Cooper-Maserati), Moises Solana in another Lotus 49, Jo Siffert (Cooper), John Surtees in the white Honda, Mike Spence and Chris Irwin in two more BRMs, Jo Bonnier in the red Cooper, Jacky Ickx (works Cooper) and Guy Ligier (Brabham). The car only just crossing the startline is Jean-Pierre Beltoise's Formula 2 Matra. This time the Lotus drivers outran the Brabhams and they finished 1–2, Jim ahead despite nursing his car through the final two laps with the right rear wheel at a weird angle due to a broken suspension mount.

ABOVE Jim leads Pedro Rodriguez's Cooper and Mike Spence's BRM, having lapped them both, through the ess on the Mexico City circuit. He qualified on the pole, took the lead on the third lap, and won as he pleased from the new BT24-Repcos of Jack Brabham and Denny Hulme. It was a great way to finish a frustrating season that had produced six pole positions, four wins and five DNFs. For Hulme, whose Brabham had delivered two wins but only two DNFs, third place here clinched the title.

ABOVE News of Jim's relocation to Bermuda captured the attention of the American motor racing community, and he received several offers of drives in the USA. One he accepted, purely out of curiosity, came from NASCAR president Bill France, who telephoned with the bait of a race at Rockingham, North Carolina. The car was a Ford Fairlane, race-prepared by Holman & Moody, and Jim could not resist. A road wheel parted company with the car during qualifying, which caused a spin and relegated him to 24th on the 44-car grid. Undeterred, he went to 12th position in the American 500 before quarter-distance, and is pictured passing Wendell Scott's Ford on the outside. Then the 7-litre V8 blew up. The race was won by Bobby Allison in another Holman & Moody Ford. *(Photo courtesy of Ed Heuvink)*

RIGHT Jim ended his season with a startling drive in a USAC Vollstedt in an invitation event at Riverside, California. It was the first time he had raced an open-wheel car that had not been built by Lotus since first sampling a single-seater, a Formula Junior Gemini, on Boxing Day 1959. Jim tried an aerofoil on the engine cover of Rolla Vollstedt's quad-cam Ford powered car and caused a sensation by putting it second on the grid next to Dan Gurney's Eagle, ahead of Lolas driven by Bobby Unser and John Surtees, AJ Foyt's Coyote and Mario Andretti's Brawner. Jim fought Dan hard for the lead of the Rex Mays 300 until Dan made a mistake and Jim took the lead – only to miss a shift and damage the engine. Unsurprisingly, Jim had predicted such an outcome in practice, when he pointed out that the gearshift throw needed to be shortened. Contrary to popular conception, he was a brilliant development driver. Gurney won from Unser and Andretti. *(Photo courtesy of Bob Tronolone)*

1968

A DREADFUL DAY AT HOCKENHEIM

The start of the new season made Jim the strong favourite to win his third World Championship. A crushing performance with the Lotus 49 delivered the opening Grand Prix in South Africa. From there, Jim flew east, and won his third Tasman title with a 49 and a downsized Cosworth V8. After a trip to Indianapolis to try the all-new, turbine-powered Lotus 56 USAC car, Jim returned to Europe for the season-opening Formula 2 race in Barcelona. The following week, Ford wanted him and Graham Hill to race the new F3L sports-prototype at Brands Hatch, but a contractual commitment sent them to a Formula 2 race at Hockenheim. Jim lost his life there. The accident, which has never been satisfactorily explained, devastated the motor racing community and his many thousands of fans all over the world.

RIGHT The end of an era. Jim achieved his 25th World Championship victory (from 72 starts) in South Africa, breaking a record held by Juan Manuel Fangio. It was his 48th Formula 1 win in total, and his last. He and Graham Hill put the Lotus 49s on the front row at Kyalami – Jim more than 6sec under the lap record to gain his 33rd pole position – and ran 1–2 all the way.

ABOVE Colin Chapman, Jack Brabham and Jim bring in the New Year after the first day of Formula 1 practice at Kyalami.

RIGHT Unfamiliar in white flat cap and sunglasses, Jim climbs aboard a Rolls-Royce for the drivers' parade at Kyalami.

NEXT SPREAD Equipped with a so-called Lotus 49T, powered by a 2.5-litre DFW version of Cosworth's Formula 1 engine, Jim was on pole position for both the opening races in the Tasman Series in New Zealand, at Pukekohe and here at Levin, the 49T's last race in green and yellow. Chris Amon's Ferrari 246 won them both, with the Lotus parked. Jim bounced back with four wins (at Christchurch, Surfers Paradise, Warwick Farm and Sandown) and took his third Tasman title 44–36. Jim is shown at the apex of the hairpin, perfectly managing the load through feet and fingertips.

ABOVE The new Team Lotus colour scheme caused a sensation when it was unveiled in New Zealand prior to the Christchurch round of the 1968 Tasman Series. It was not the first team to have a title sponsor, but this was a tobacco brand, and the cars were painted white, red and gold like the cigarette packet. Jim won the first event contested by Gold Leaf Team Lotus but never did race a Formula 1 car in these colours.

RIGHT Jim qualified his Formula 2 Lotus 48 second on the grid in Montjuich Park, in the hills above Barcelona, only a tenth of second shy of Jackie Stewart in Ken Tyrrell's Matra MS7, while Graham Hill struggled with the sister car, lining up 13th. On the second lap, Jim was rammed from behind under braking at the hairpin by Jacky Ickx's Ferrari, putting them both out of the race. Stewart won. Jim was unusually furious with Ickx, ticking off the young Belgian in a way he never forgot...

LEFT Jim corners during the fateful Formula 2 race on 7 April. The Gold Leaf Lotus 48s were curiously off the pace in the Deutschland Trophy. Jim was running eighth on the fifth lap of the first heat when he crashed at 140mph on a remote section of the Hockenheimring. The only eyewitness was a marshal, some distance away, who reported that the Lotus seemed to twitch, straighten out again, and then spear off the track and into the trees. There were no barriers there. The car disintegrated and Jim was killed instantly. Graham Hill, unaware of the extent of the tragedy, finished the heat in 12th position, and then Team Lotus packed up and made their way home. A subsequent investigation concluded that Jim's Lotus had run over a piece of debris on the track, causing the Firestone slowly to deflate and throw him into a slide on the flat-out right-hander. After Jim's accident, all tyre manufacturers began to fit safety bolts to ensure that their tyres did not leave the rim in the event of a deflation.

ABOVE A throng of shocked motor racing people went to Scotland for Jim's funeral at Chirnside Old Church, near his farm at Duns, Berwickshire, the Wednesday after his death. The church could hold only 600 mourners and a loudspeaker system relayed the service to many times that number who paid their tributes to him outside. His grave lies next to that of his mother, Helen.

RACE RESULTS

Compiled by David Hayhoe

1956

Date	Country/event	Circuit	Car	Model	Engine	Configuration	Notes	Result
03/06	Saloon Cars over 2,000cc (sprint)	Stobs Camp	Sunbeam	Mk3	Sunbeam	4	only finisher	1PRIVATE
16/06	Sports Cars under 1,200cc	Crimond	DKW	Sonderklasse	DKW	3	first circuit race	8
30/09	Saloon Cars under 1,200cc (sprint)	Winfield	DKW	Sonderklasse	DKW	3		1
	Modified Saloons under 1,500cc (sprint)	Winfield	DKW	Sonderklasse	DKW	3		1
	Saloons unlimited (sprint)	Winfield	Sunbeam	Mk3	Sunbeam	4		1
	Modified Saloons unlimited (sprint)	Winfield	Sunbeam	Mk3	Sunbeam	4		1
07/10	High Speed Trials	Brunton Beadnell	DKW	Sonderklasse	DKW	3	1st in class	6
			Sunbeam	Mk3	Sunbeam	4	1st in class	6

1957

Date	Country/event	Circuit	Car	Model	Engine	Configuration	Notes	Result
30/06	Production Cars Handicap	Charterhall	DKW	Sonderklasse	DKW	3		4
01/09	Sports Cars 1,500-2,700cc	Charterhall	Sunbeam	Mk3	Sunbeam	4		8
05/10	Production Sports Cars Handicap	Charterhall	Porsche	1600S	Porsche	4		3
	Production Touring Cars Handicap	Charterhall	Porsche	1600S	Porsche	4		2
	BMRC Trophy	Charterhall	Porsche	1600S	Porsche	4	first circuit win	1
06/10	Modified Saloons unlimited (sprint)	Winfield	Porsche	1600S	Porsche	4	dead heat with Ian Scott-Watson	1
	Sports Cars 1,500-3,000cc (sprint)	Winfield	Porsche	1600S	Porsche	4		2

1958

Date	Country/event	Circuit	Car	Model	Engine	Configuration	Notes	Result
05/04	Racing Cars over 500cc	Full Sutton	Jaguar	D Type	Jaguar	6		1
	Sports Cars unlimited	Full Sutton	Jaguar	D Type	Jaguar	6		1
	Production Sports Cars unlimited	Full Sutton	Porsche	1600S	Porsche	4		6
20/04	Saloon Cars under 2,000cc (sprint)	Winfield	Porsche	1600S	Porsche	4		1
	Sports Cars unlimited	Winfield	Porsche	1600S	Porsche	4		2
27/04	Formule Libre	Charterhall	Jaguar	D Type	Jaguar	6		8
	Sports Cars 1,500-3,000cc	Charterhall	Porsche	1600S	Porsche	4		4
	Sports Cars under 2,000cc	Charterhall	Porsche	1600S	Porsche	4	puncture	r
18/05	Spa Grand Prix (over 1,500cc)	Spa-Francorchamps	Jaguar	D Type	Jaguar	6	first foreign race	8
	GT Specials under 2,000cc	Spa-Francorchamps	Porsche	1600S	Porsche	4		5
24/05	Sports Cars unlimited	Full Sutton	Jaguar	D Type	Jaguar	6		1
	Formule Libre	Full Sutton	Jaguar	D Type	Jaguar	6		1
	Saloon & GT Cars unlimited	Full Sutton	Porsche	1600S	Porsche	4		1
08/06	Sports Cars under 2,000cc (sprint)	Stobs Camp	Porsche	1600S	Porsche	4		1
			Triumph	TR3	Triumph	4		2
21/06	Sports Cars unlimited	Crimond	Jaguar	D Type	Jaguar	6		1
	Sports Cars 1,500-3,000cc	Crimond	Porsche	1600S	Porsche	4		4
	Invitation Handicap	Crimond	Jaguar	D Type	Jaguar	6		8
28/06	Production Sports Cars 1,500-2,000cc	Rest And Be Thankful	Porsche	1600S	Porsche	4	first hill climb	1
			Triumph	TR3	Triumph	4		3
29/06	Formule Libre	Charterhall	Jaguar	D Type	Jaguar	6		1
	Sports Cars unlimited	Charterhall	Jaguar	D Type	Jaguar	6		1
05/07	Sports Cars 1,500-2,000cc	Rest And Be Thankful	Porsche	1600S	Porsche	4		1
			Triumph	TR3	Triumph	4		2
06/07	Racing Cars Handicap	Charterhall	Jaguar	D Type	Jaguar	6		1
	Touring Cars Handicap	Charterhall	Porsche	1600S	Porsche	4		2
	Production Sports Cars Handicap	Charterhall	Porsche	1600S	Porsche	4		4
	BMRC Trophy Handicap	Charterhall	Jaguar	D Type	Jaguar	6		2
12/07	Formule Libre	Full Sutton	Jaguar	D Type	Jaguar	6		1
	Sports Cars over 1,500cc	Full Sutton	Jaguar	D Type	Jaguar	6		1
	Production. Sports Cars under 1,600cc	Full Sutton	Porsche	1600S	Porsche	4		1
27/07	Mod. Touring Cars over 1,500cc (sprint)	Winfield	Porsche	1600S	Porsche	4		1
	Sports Cars 1,500-3,000cc (sprint)	Winfield	Porsche	1600S	Porsche	4		1
	Sports/Racing Cars unlimited (sprint)	Winfield	Jaguar	D Type	Jaguar	6		1
04/08	Sports Cars over 1,500cc	Mallory Park	Jaguar	D Type	Jaguar	6		1
	Formule Libre Heat	Mallory Park	Jaguar	D Type	Jaguar	6		2
	Formule Libre Final	Mallory Park	Jaguar	D Type	Jaguar	6		7
16/08	Six Hours Relay Race (handicap)	Silverstone	Porsche	1600S	Porsche	4		22
28/09	Formule Libre	Charterhall	Jaguar	D Type	Jaguar	6		2
	Sports Cars over 1,500cc	Charterhall	Jaguar	D Type	Jaguar	6		3
	Production Sports Cars under 1,600cc	Charterhall	Porsche	1600S	Porsche	4		3
26/12	GT Cars unlimited	Brands Hatch	Lotus	Elite	Climax	4		2

1959

Date	Country/event	Circuit	Car	Model	Engine	Configuration	Notes	Result
30/03	GT Cars 1,000 1,600 cc	Mallory Park	Lotus	Elite	Climax	4		1
	Sports Cars over 1,200cc	Mallory Park	Lister Jaguar		Jaguar	6		1
	Formule Libre Heat	Mallory Park	Lister Jaguar		Jaguar	6		1
	Formule Libre Final	Mallory Park	Lister Jaguar		Jaguar	6		1
11/04	Sports Cars under 1,500cc	Oulton Park	Lotus	Elite	Climax	4		10
	Sports Cars over 1,500cc	Oulton Park	Lister Jaguar		Jaguar	6		8
18/04	Sports Cars over 1,500cc	Aintree	Lister Jaguar		Jaguar	6		6
25/04	Sports Cars over 2,000cc	Charterhall	Lister Jaguar		Jaguar	6		1
	Formule Libre	Charterhall	Lister Jaguar		Jaguar	6		1
	GT Cars under 1,600cc	Charterhall	Porsche	1600S	Porsche	4		2
18/05	Whitsun Trophy (Sports Cars)	Goodwood	Lister Jaguar		Jaguar	6	out of fuel	r
30/05	Sports Cars unlimited	Rufforth	Lister Jaguar		Jaguar	6		1
	Formula Libre	Rufforth	Lister Jaguar		Jaguar	6		2
07/06	GT Cars under 1,600cc (sprint)	Stobs Camp	Porsche	1600S	Porsche	4		1
	Sports Cars unlimited (sprint)	Stobs Camp	Porsche	1600S	Porsche	4		1
20-21/06	Le Mans 24 Hours	Le Mans	Lotus	Elite	Climax	4	2nd in 1,500cc class (co: J Whitmore)	10
05/07	GT World Cup Race	Zandvoort	Lotus	Elite	Climax	4	rear axle	r
11/07	Sports Cars over 2,000cc	Bo'ness	Lister Jaguar		Jaguar	6	hill climb	1
	Sports Cars under 1,600cc	Bo'ness	Lotus	Elite	Climax	4	hill climb	2
			Porsche	1600S	Porsche	4	hill climb	7
18/07	Sports Cars over 2,000cc	Aintree	Lister Jaguar		Jaguar	6		2
26/07	Sports Cars over 1,500cc (sprint)	Winfield	Lister Jaguar		Jaguar	6		1
	GT Cars 1,000-2,000cc	Winfield	Lotus	Elite	Climax	4		1
			Porsche	1600S	Porsche	4		2
	Formule Libre (sprint)	Winfield	Lister Jaguar		Jaguar	6		1
02/08	Formule Libre Heat	Mallory Park	Lister Jaguar		Jaguar	6		3
	Formule Libre Final	Mallory Park	Lister Jaguar		Jaguar	6		4
	Sports Cars over 1,200cc Heat	Mallory Park	Lister Jaguar		Jaguar	6		2
	Sports Cars over 1,200cc Final	Mallory Park	Lister Jaguar		Jaguar	6		2
	GT Cars up to 1,600cc	Mallory Park	Lotus	Elite	Climax	4		2
18/08	Tourist Trophy	Goodwood	Tojeiro Jaguar		Jaguar	6	crashed by co-driver Masten Gregory	r
29/08	GT World Cup Race Heat 1	Brands Hatch	Lotus	Elite	Climax	4		1
	GT World Cup Race Heat 2	Brands Hatch	Lotus	Elite	Climax	4		2
	Sports Cars over 3,000cc	Brands Hatch	Lister Jaguar		Jaguar	6		1
13/09	Sports Cars over 1,200cc	Mallory Park	Lister Jaguar		Jaguar	6		1
	Formule Libre Heat	Mallory Park	Lister Jaguar		Jaguar	6		3
	Formule Libre Final	Mallory Park	Lister Jaguar		Jaguar	6		8
	GT Cars 1,000-1,600cc	Mallory Park	Lotus	Elite	Climax	4		1
26/09	GT Cars under 1,600cc	Oulton Park	Lotus	Elite	Climax	4		1
27/09	Sports Cars over 1,500cc	Charterhall	Lister Jaguar		Jaguar	6	dropped valve	r
	Sports Cars under 1,300cc	Charterhall	Lotus	Elite	Climax	4		5
	GT Cars unlimited	Charterhall	Lotus	Elite	Climax	4		1
04/10	Sports Cars over 1,500cc	Charterhall	Lister Jaguar		Jaguar	6		1
	Formule Libre	Charterhall	Lister Jaguar		Jaguar	6		1
	GT Cars unlimited	Charterhall	Lotus	Elite	Climax	4		1
	Sports Cars under 1,300cc	Charterhall	Lotus	Elite	Climax	4		4
	BMRC Trophy Handicap	Charterhall	Lister Jaguar		Jaguar	6		13
10/10	Snetterton 3 Hours	Snetterton	Lotus	Elite	Climax	4		1
26/12	GT Cars unlimited	Brands Hatch	Lotus	Elite	Climax	4	accident	r
	Formula Junior	Brands Hatch	Gemini	Mk2	Austin	4	first single-seat race/ flat battery	r

1960

Date	Country/event	Circuit	Car	Model	Engine	Configuration	Notes	Grid position	Result
19/03	Formula Junior	Goodwood	FJ Lotus	18	Ford Cosworth	4	fastest lap		1
02/04	Formula Junior	Oulton Park	FJ Lotus	18	Ford Cosworth	4	fastest lap		1
	Sports Cars over 1,100cc	Oulton Park	Aston Martin	DBR1/300	Aston Martin	6			3
10/04	Brussels Grand Prix Heat 1	Heysel	F2 Lotus	18	Climax	4	engine	5	r
16/04	Formula Junior	Goodwood	FJ Lotus	18	Ford Cosworth	4	fastest lap		1
	Sports Cars unlimited	Goodwood	Aston Martin	DBR1/300	Aston Martin	6	fuel starvation		r
30/04	BARC 200	Aintree	F2 Lotus	18	Climax	4	Innes Ireland took over		9
	BARC 200 Formula Junior	Aintree	FJ Lotus	18	Ford Cosworth	4	throttle stuck/ accident/ fastest lap		r
14/05	Formula Junior	Silverstone	FJ Lotus	18	Ford Cosworth	4			1
	Sports Cars unlimited	Silverstone	Aston Martin	DBR1/300	Aston Martin	6	throttle linkage		r
22/05	Nürburgring 1,000km	Nürburgring	Aston Martin	DBR1/300	Aston Martin	6	engine/ co: Roy Salvadori		r
27/05	Formula Junior	Monte-Carlo	FJ Lotus	18	Ford Cosworth	4	ignition/ fastest lap	1	17
06/06	DUTCH GP	Zandvoort	F1 Lotus	18	Climax	4	first WC F1 race/ transmission	11	r
19/06	BELGIAN GP	Spa-Francorchamps	F1 Lotus	18	Climax	4		9	5
25-26/06	Le Mans 24 Hours	Le Mans	Aston Martin	DBR1/300	Aston Martin	6	co: Roy Salvadori		3
03/07	FRENCH GP	Reims-Gueux	F1 Lotus	18	Climax	4		12	5
16/07	BRITISH GP	Silverstone	F1 Lotus	18	Climax	4		8	16
24/07	Solitude Grand Prix	Solitude	F2 Lotus	18	Climax	4		1	8
	Formula Junior	Solitude	FJ Lotus	18	Ford Cosworth	4	fastest lap		1
01/08	Silver City Trophy	Brands Hatch	F1 Lotus	18	Climax	4	transmission/ fastest lap	1	r
	Formula Junior	Brands Hatch	FJ Lotus	18	Ford Cosworth	4	fastest lap	1	1
14/08	PORTUGUESE GP	Porto	F1 Lotus	18	Climax	4		8	3
19/08	BARC FJ Championship Heat 2	Goodwood	FJ Lotus	18	Ford Cosworth	4	fastest lap		1
	BARC FJ Championship Final	Goodwood	FJ Lotus	18	Ford Cosworth	4			2
27/08	Kentish Hundred	Brands Hatch	F2 Lotus	18	Climax	4			1
	Formula Junior	Brands Hatch	FJ Lotus	18	Ford Cosworth	4			2
17/09	Lombank Trophy	Snetterton	F1 Lotus	18	Climax	4	Fastest lap		2
	Formula Junior	Snetterton	FJ Lotus	18	Ford Cosworth	4			2
24/09	International Gold Cup	Oulton Park	F1 Lotus	18	Climax	4	accident/ fastest lap	2	r
	Formula Junior Heat 1	Oulton Park	FJ Lotus	18	Ford Cosworth	4		1	1
	Formula Junior Heat 2	Oulton Park	FJ Lotus	18	Ford Cosworth	4		1	1
	Formula Junior Aggregate	Oulton Park	FJ Lotus	18	Ford Cosworth	4			1
25/09	Formule Libre	Charterhall	FJ Lotus	18	Ford Cosworth	4	transmission		r
24/10	Lewis-Evans Trophy	Brands Hatch	FJ Lotus	18	Ford Cosworth	4	FJ lap record (with Arundell)		2
24/10	GT over 3000cc	Brands Hatch	Austin Healey	3000	BMC	6			1
31/10	Paris 1,000km	Montlhéry	Aston Martin	DBR1/300	Aston Martin	6	engine/ co: Tony Maggs		r
20/11	UNITED STATES GP	Riverside	F1 Lotus	18	Climax	4	accident	5	16
26/12	John Davy Trophy	Brands Hatch	FJ Lotus	18	Ford Cosworth	4	fastest lap		1

1961

Date	Country/event	Circuit	Car	Model	Engine	Configuration	Notes	Grid position	Result
07/01	New Zealand Grand Prix	Ardmore	F Int. Lotus	18	Climax	4		11	6
14/01	Levin International	Levin	F Int. Lotus	18	Climax	4			2
21/01	Lady Wigram Trophy	Christchurch	F Int. Lotus	18	Climax	4	spin	1	r
26/03	Lombank Trophy	Snetterton	F1 Lotus	18	Climax	4	4th in F1 class	6	6
03/04	Pau Grand Prix	Pau	F1 Lotus	18	Climax	4	fastest lap	2	1
08/04	Brussels Grand Prix Heat 1	Heysel	F1 Lotus	18	Climax	4	gearbox	6	r
22/04	BARC 200	Aintree	F1 Lotus	18	Climax	4		5	9
26/04	Syracuse Grand Prix	Siracusa, Sicily	F1 Lotus	18	Climax	4		12	6
06/05	International Trophy	Silverstone	F Int. Lotus	18	Climax	4			8
14/05	MONACO GP	Monte-Carlo	F1 Lotus	21	Climax	4		3	10
22/05	DUTCH GP	Zandvoort	F1 Lotus	21	Climax	4	fastest lap	10	3
28/05	Nürburgring 1,000km	Nürburgring	Aston Martin	DBR1/300	Aston Martin	6	co: Bruce McLaren/ engine		r
03/06	Silver City Trophy	Brands Hatch	F1 Lotus	21	Climax	4		3	2
09-10/06	Le Mans 24 Hours	Le Mans	Aston Martin	DBR1/300	Aston Martin	6	clutch/ co: Ron Flockhart		r
18/06	BELGIAN GP	Spa-Francorchamps	F1 Lotus	21	Climax	4		16	12
02/07	FRENCH GP	Reims-Gueux	F1 Lotus	21	Climax	4		5	3
09/07	British Empire Trophy	Silverstone	F Int. Lotus	18	Climax	4			5
15/07	BRITISH GP	Aintree	F1 Lotus	21	Climax	4	oil line	8	r
23/07	Solitude Grand Prix	Solitude	F1 Lotus	21	Climax	4		7	7
06/08	GERMAN GP	Nürburgring	F1 Lotus	21	Climax	4		8	4
07/08	Guards Trophy	Brands Hatch	F Int. Lotus	18	Climax	4			2
19/08	Tourist Trophy	Goodwood	Aston Martin	DB4GT Zagato	Aston Martin	6		4	
20/08	Kanonloppet	Karlskoga, Sweden	F1 Lotus	21	Climax	4	suspension/ oil tank	1	r
26/08	Danish Grand Prix Heat 1	Roskildering	F1 Lotus	18	Climax	4		11	6
27/08	Danish Grand Prix Heat 2	Roskildering	F1 Lotus	18	Climax	4	steering		r
	Danish Grand Prix Heat 3	Roskildering	F1 Lotus	18	Climax	4			4
26-27/08	Danish Grand PrixAggregate	Roskildering	F1 Lotus	18	Climax	4		11	7
03/09	Modena Grand Prix	Modena	F1 Lotus	21	Climax	4		6	4
10/09	ITALIAN GP	Monza	F1 Lotus	21	Climax	4	accident	7	r
17/09	Flugplatzrennen	Zeltweg	F1 Lotus	21	Climax	4		2	4
23/09	International Gold Cup	Oulton Park	F1 Lotus	21	Climax	4	rear suspension	4	r
24/09	Formule Libre	Charterhall	Aston Martin	DBR1/300	Aston Martin	6			2
	Sports Cars unlimited	Charterhall	Aston Martin	DBR1/300	Aston Martin	6			2
08/10	UNITED STATES GP	Watkins Glen	F1 Lotus	21	Climax	4	5	7	
15/10	Paris 1,000km	Montlhéry	Aston Martin	DB4GT Zagato	Aston Martin	6	co: Innes Ireland	6	
09/12	Rand Grand Prix	Kyalami	F1 Lotus	21	Climax	4		1	1
17/12	Natal Grand Prix	Westmead, Durban	F1 Lotus	21	Climax	4		1	1
26/12	South African Grand Prix	East London	F1 Lotus	21	Climax	4	fastest lap	1	

1962

Date	Country/event	Circuit	Car	Model	Engine	Configuration	Notes	Grid position	Result
01/01	Cape Grand Prix	Killarney	F1 Lotus	21	Climax	4	fastest lap	1	2
11/02	Inter-continental GT, 1,300cc class	Daytona	Lotus	Elite	Climax	4			4
12/03	Sandown Park International Heat	Sandown Park, Melbourne	F Int. Lotus	21	Climax	4			2
	Sandown Park International Final	Sandown Park, Melbourne	F Int. Lotus	21	Climax	4			6
01/04	Brussels Grand Prix Heat 1	Heysel	F1 Lotus	24	Climax	V8	engine valve	1	r
14/04	Lombank Trophy	Snetterton	F1 Lotus	24	Climax	V8		2	1
23/04	Pau Grand Prix	Pau	F1 Lotus	24	Climax	V8	gear selectors/ fastest lap	1	r
28/04	BARC 200	Aintree	F1 Lotus	24	Climax	V8	fastest lap	1	1
12/05	International Trophy	Silverstone	F1 Lotus	24	Climax	V8	fastest lap	2	2
	GT Cars unlimited	Silverstone	Aston Martin	DBR1/300	Aston Martin	6			3
20/05	DUTCH GP	Zandvoort	F1 Lotus	25	Climax	V8		3	9 PRIVATE
27/05	Nürburgring 1,000 Km	Nürburgring	Lotus	23	Ford Cosworth	4	co: T Taylor/ exhaust leak/ accident	7	r
03/06	MONACO GP	Monte-Carlo	F1 Lotus	25	Climax	V8	clutch/ first WC F1 pole/ fastest lap	1	r
11/06	International 2,000 Guineas	Mallory Park	F1 Lotus	25	Climax	V8	oil pressure	1	r
17/06	BELGIAN GP	Spa-Francorchamps	F1 Lotus	25	Climax	V8	fastest lap	12	1
01/07	Reims Grand Prix	Reims-Gueux	F1 Lotus	25	Climax	V8	header tank/ overheating	1	r
			F1 Lotus	24	BRM	V8	out of fuel/ Peter Arundell's car		r
08/07	FRENCH GP	Rouen-les-Essarts	F1 Lotus	25	Climax	V8	front suspension/ fastest lap	1	r
15/07	Solitude Grand Prix	Solitude	F1 Lotus	25	Climax	V8	accident	1	r
21/07	BRITISH GP	Aintree	F1 Lotus	25	Climax	V8	fastest lap	1	1
05/08	GERMAN GP	Nürburgring	F1 Lotus	25	Climax	V8		3	4
06/08	Guards Trophy	Brands Hatch	Lotus	23	Ford Cosworth	4	clutch		r
18/08	Tourist Trophy	Goodwood	Aston Martin	DB4GT Zagato	Aston Martin	6	accident		r
26/08	Swiss Mountain Grand Prix	Ollon Villars	F1 Lotus	21	Climax	4	hill climb/ 3rd in class		nc
01/09	Sports Cars up to 1,600cc	Oulton Park	Lotus	23	Ford Cosworth	4			2
	International Gold Cup	Oulton Park	F1 Lotus	25	Climax	V8	fastest lap	2	1
16/09	ITALIAN GP	Monza	F1 Lotus	25	Climax	V8	transmission	1	r
29/09	Autosport 3 Hours	Snetterton	Lotus	23	Ford Cosworth	4	pushstart	2	dq
07/10	UNITED STATES GP	Watkins Glen	F1 Lotus	25	Climax	V8	fastest lap	1	1
21/10	Paris 1,000km	Montlhéry	Aston Martin	DB4GT Zagato	Aston Martin	6	engine/co:John Whitmore	6	r
04/11	Mexican Grand Prix	Mexico City	F1 Lotus	25	Climax	V8	pushstart	1	dq
			F1 Lotus	25	Climax	V8	Trevor Taylor's car/ fastest lap		1
15/12	Rand Grand Prix	Kyalami	F1 Lotus	25	Climax	V8	fastest lap	1	1
22/12	Natal Grand Prix Heat 1	Westmead, Durban	F1 Lotus	25	Climax	V8		1	12
	Natal Grand Prix Final	Westmead, Durban	F1 Lotus	25	Climax	V8		22	2
29/12	SOUTH AFRICAN GP	East London	F1 Lotus	25	Climax	V8	oil leak/ fastest lap	1	r

1963

Date	Country/event	Circuit	Car	Model	Engine	Configuration	Notes	Grid position	Result
30/03	Lombank Trophy	Snetterton	F1 Lotus	25	Climax	V8		1	2
06/04	British Empire Trophy	Oulton Park	Lotus	23B	Ford Cosworth	4			1
15/04	Pau Grand Prix	Pau	F1 Lotus	25	Climax	V8	fastest lap	1	1
21/04	Imola Grand Prix	Castellacis, Italy	F1 Lotus	25	Climax	V8		1	1
27/04	BARC 200	Aintree	F1 Lotus	25	Climax	V8	Trevor Taylor took over	1	7
			F1 Lotus	25	Climax	V8	Taylor's car/ fastest lap		3
11/05	International Trophy	Silverstone	F1 Lotus	25	Climax	V8		6	1
26/05	MONACO GP	Monte-Carlo	F1 Lotus	25	Climax	V8	gear selector/ accident	1	8r
30/05	Indianapolis 500	Indianapolis	USAC Lotus	29	Ford Fairlane	V8		5	2
01/06	Player's 200	Mosport Park	Lotus	23B	Ford Cosworth	4	3rd in class		8
03/06	Sports Cars unlimited	Crystal Palace	Lotus	23B	Ford Cosworth	4			1
09/06	BELGIAN GP	Spa-Francorchamps	F1 Lotus	25	Climax	V8	fastest lap	8	1
23/06	DUTCH GP	Zandvoort	F1 Lotus	25	Climax	V8	fastest lap	1	1
30/06	FRENCH GP	Reims-Gueux	F1 Lotus	25	Climax	V8	fastest lap	1	1
20/07	BRITISH GP	Silverstone	F1 Lotus	25	Climax	V8		1	1
28/07	Solitude Grand Prix	Solitude	F1 Lotus	25	Climax	V8	fastest lap	1	nc
04/08	GERMAN GP	Nürburgring	F1 Lotus	25	Climax	V8		1	2
05/08	Slip Molyslip Trophy	Brands Hatch	Ford	Galaxie	Ford	V8			1
11/08	Kanonloppet Heat 1	Karlskoga, Sweden	F1 Lotus	25	Climax	V8	fastest lap	2	1
	Kanonloppet Heat 2	Karlskoga, Sweden	F1 Lotus	25	Climax	V8		1	3
	Kanonloppet Aggregate	Karlskoga, Sweden	F1 Lotus	25	Climax	V8			1
18/08	Milwaukee 200	Milwaukee	USAC Lotus	29	Ford Fairlane	V8		1	1
01/09	Austrian Grand Prix	Zeltweg	F1 Lotus	25	Climax	V8	oil pipe	1	r
08/09	ITALIAN GP	Monza	F1 Lotus	25	Climax	V8	fastest lap/ clinched F1 world title	3	1
21/09	International Gold Cup	Oulton Park	F1 Lotus	25	Climax	V8	fastest lap	1	1
	Sports Cars up to 2,000cc	Oulton Park	Lotus	23B	Ford Cosworth	4			1
22/09	Trenton 200 State Fair Race	Trenton	USAC Lotus	29	Ford Fairlane	V8	oil leak	1	r
28/09	Snetterton 3 Hours	Snetterton	Lotus	23B	Ford Cosworth	4			1
	Saloon Cars unlimited	Snetterton	Lotus Cortina		Lotus	4			2
06/10	UNITED STATES GP	Watkins Glen	F1 Lotus	25	Climax	V8	stalled on grid/ fastest lap	2	3
13/10	Riverside Grand Prix	Riverside	Lotus	23B	Ford Cosworth	4	1st in class		5
20/10	Monterey Grand Prix	Laguna Seca	Lotus	19	Climax	4	oil cooler		r
27/10	MEXICAN GP	Mexico City	F1 Lotus	25	Climax	V8	fastest lap	1	1
14/12	Rand Grand Prix Heat 1	Kyalami	F1 Lotus	25	Climax	V8		4	19
	Rand Grand Prix Heat 2	Kyalami	F1 Lotus	25	Climax	V8			5
	Rand Grand Prix Aggregate	Kyalami	F1 Lotus	25	Climax	V8			16
28/12	SOUTH AFRICAN GP	East London	F1 Lotus	25	Climax	V8		1	1

1964

Date	Country/event	Circuit	Car	Model	Engine	Configuration	Notes	Grid position	Result
14/03	Daily Mirror Trophy	Snetterton	F1 Lotus	25	Climax	V8	ignition waterlogged	1	r
	Saloon Cars unlimited	Snetterton	Lotus Cortina		Lotus	4	1st in class		2
22/03	Saloon Cars unlimited	Sebring	Lotus Cortina		Lotus	4	1st in class		3
23/03	Sebring 12 Hours	Sebring	Lotus Cortina		Lotus	4	2nd in class/ co: Ray Parsons		21
30/03	News of the World Trophy	Goodwood	F1 Lotus	25	Climax	V8		2	1
	St. Mary's Trophy	Goodwood	Lotus Cortina		Lotus	4	1st & fastest lap in class		2
05/04	Pau Grand Prix	Pau	F2 Lotus	32	Ford Cosworth	4	fastest lap	1	1
11/04	Saloon Cars unlimited	Oulton Park	Lotus Cortina		Lotus	4	fastest lap		1
			Lotus	19	Climax	4	fastest lap		1
	GT Cars up to 2,500cc	Oulton Park	Lotus	Elan	Lotus Ford	4	fastest lap		1
18/04	BARC 200	Aintree	F1 Lotus	25	Climax	V8	accident/ fastest lap	4	r
	Sports Cars unlimited	Aintree	Lotus	30	Ford Fairlane	V8	1st & fastest lap in class		2
	Saloon Cars unlimited	Aintree	Lotus Cortina		Lotus	4	1st & fastest lap in class		3
26/04	Eifelrennen	Nürburgring	F2 Lotus	32	Ford Cosworth	4	fastest lap	1	1
02/05	International Trophy	Silverstone	F1 Lotus	25	Climax	V8	valve springs	4	r
	GT Cars unlimited	Silverstone	Lotus	Elan	Lotus Ford	4	1st & fastest lap in class		10
	Sports Cars unlimited	Silverstone	Lotus	30	Ford Fairlane	V8	fuel injection		ns
	Saloon Cars unlimited	Silverstone	Lotus Cortina		Lotus	4	1st & fastest lap in class		3
10/05	MONACO GP	Monte-Carlo	F1 Lotus	25	Climax	V8	oil pressure	1	4r
16/05	Grovewood Trophy	Mallory Park	F2 Lotus	32	Ford Cosworth	4	fastest lap	3	1
	Sports Cars over 2,000cc	Mallory Park	Lotus	30	Ford Fairlane	V8	fastest lap	1	1
18/05	London Trophy Heat 1	Crystal Palace	F2 Lotus	32	Ford Cosworth	4		7	2
	London Trophy Final	Crystal Palace	F2 Lotus	32	Ford Cosworth	4		4	10
	Saloon Cars over 1,300cc	Crystal Palace	Lotus Cortina		Lotus	4			1
24/05	DUTCH GP	Zandvoort	F1 Lotus	25	Climax	V8	fastest lap	2	1
30/05	Indianapolis 500	Indianapolis	USAC Lotus	34	Ford	V8	rear suspension	1	24r
14/06	BELGIAN GP	Spa-Francorchamps	F1 Lotus	25	Climax	V8		6	1
28/06	FRENCH GP	Rouen-les-Essarts	F1 Lotus	25	Climax	V8	piston	1	r
05/07	Reims Grand Prix	Reims-Gueux	F2 Lotus	32	Ford Cosworth	4		6	4
11/07	BRITISH GP	Brands Hatch	F1 Lotus	25	Climax	V8	fastest lap	1	1
19/07	Solitude Grand Prix	Solitude	F1 Lotus	25	Climax	V8	fastest lap	1	1
02/08	GERMAN GP	Nürburgring	F1 Lotus	25	Climax	V8	valve gear	2	r
03/08	British Eagle Trophy	Brands Hatch	F2 Lotus	32	Ford Cosworth	4		2	r
	Guards Trophy	Brands Hatch	Lotus	30	Ford Fairlane	V8	fuel pump on grid		r
	Saloon Cars unlimited	Brands Hatch	Lotus Cortina		Lotus	4	1st in class		2
09/08	Kanonloppet Heat 1	Karlskoga, Sweden	F2 Lotus	32	Ford Cosworth	4		1	1
	Kanonloppet Final	Karlskoga, Sweden	F2 Lotus	32	Ford Cosworth	4		1	2
16/08	Mediterranean Grand Prix	Enna, Sicily	F1 Lotus	25	Climax	V8		3	2
23/08	AUSTRIAN GP	Zeltweg	F1 Lotus	33	Climax	V8		3	r
29/08	Tourist Trophy	Goodwood	Lotus	30	Ford Fairlane	V8	4th in class	2	12
06/09	ITALIAN GP	Monza	F1 Lotus	33	Climax	V8	piston	4	r
13/09	Albi Grand Prix	Albi	F2 Lotus	32	Ford Cosworth	4	engine	2	r
19/09	International Gold Cup	Oulton Park	F2 Lotus	32	Ford Cosworth	4	fastest lap	4	2
	Saloon Cars unlimited	Oulton Park	Lotus Cortina		Lotus	4	fastest lap		1
26/09	Canadian Grand Prix	Mosport Park	Lotus	30	Ford Fairlane	V8	accident damage		r
27/09	Trenton 200	Trenton	USAC Lotus	34	Ford	V8	engine	6	r
04/10	UNITED STATES GP	Watkins Glen	F1 Lotus	25	Climax	V8	Spence took over/ engine	1	r
			F1 Lotus	33	Climax	V8	Spence's car/ fuel pump/ fastest lap		7r
11/10	Times Grand Prix	Riverside	Lotus	30	Ford Fairlane	V8			3
25/10	MEXICAN GP	Mexico City	F1 Lotus	33	Climax	V8	oil line/ engine/ fastest lap	1	5r

1965

Date	Country/event	Circuit	Car	Model	Engine	Configuration	Notes	Grid position	Result
01/01	SOUTH AFRICAN GP	East London	F1 Lotus	33	Climax	V8	fastest lap	1	1
09/01	New Zealand Grand Prix (Tasman) Prel	Pukekohe	F1 Lotus	32B	Climax	4		1	1
	New Zealand Grand Prix (Tasman)	Pukekohe	F1 Lotus	32B	Climax	4	accident	2	r
16/01	Gold Leaf International (Tasman) Prel	Levin	F1 Lotus	32B	Climax	4	fastest lap	1	1
	Gold Leaf International (Tasman)	Levin	F1 Lotus	32B	Climax	4	fastest lap	1	1
	Flying Farewell (Tasman)	Levin	F1 Lotus	32B	Climax	4	fastest lap	1	1
23/01	Lady Wigram Trophy (Tasman) Heat 2	Christchurch	F1 Lotus	32B	Climax	4		1	1
	Lady Wigram Trophy (Tasman) Final	Christchurch	F1 Lotus	32B	Climax	4		1	1
30/01	Teretonga Trophy (Tasman) Heat 1	Invercargill	F1 Lotus	32B	Climax	4	fastest lap	1	1
	Teretonga Trophy (Tasman) Final	Invercargill	F1 Lotus	32B	Climax	4	fastest lap	1	1
	Flying Farewell	Invercargill	F1 Lotus	32B	Climax	4		1	2
14/02	Warwick Farm International 100 (Tasman)	Warwick Farm	F1 Lotus	32B	Climax	4	fastest lap	3	1
21/02	Sandown Park International Cup (Tasman)	Sandown Park, Melb'ne	F1 Lotus	32B	Climax	4		2	2
01/03	Australian Grand Prix (Tasman) Heat	Longford, Tasmania	F1 Lotus	32B	Climax	4			5
	Australian Grand Prix (Tasman) Final	Longford, Tasmania	F1 Lotus	32B	Climax	4		4	5
07/03	Lakeside International (Tasman)	Lakeside, Brisbane	F1 Lotus	32B	Climax	4	fastest lap	1	1
13/03	Daily Mail Race of Champions Heat 1	Brands Hatch	F1 Lotus	33	Climax	V8	fastest lap	1	1
	Daily Mail Race of Champions Heat 2	Brands Hatch	F1 Lotus	33	Climax	V8	accident/ fastest lap	1	r
	Daily Mail Race of Champions Aggregate	Brands Hatch	F1 Lotus	33	Climax	V8	accident/ fastest lap		r
	Saloon Cars unlimited	Brands Hatch	Lotus Cortina		Lotus	4	lost wheel/ fastest lap		r
20/03	Guards Trophy	Silverstone	Lotus	30	Ford Fairlane	V8	fastest lap	1	1
26/03	Sebring 3 Hours	Sebring	Lotus Cortina		Lotus	4	fastest lap	1	1
04/04	Syracuse Grand Prix	Siracusa, Italy	F1 Lotus	33	Climax	V8	fastest lap	1	1
10/04	Autocar Trophy Heat 1	Snetterton	F2 Lotus	32	Ford Cosworth	4	fastest lap/dead heat with G Hill		1
	Autocar Trophy Heat 2	Snetterton	F2 Lotus	32	Ford Cosworth	4			5
	Autocar Trophy Aggregate	Snetterton	F2 Lotus	32	Ford Cosworth	4			3
	Saloon Cars unlimited	Snetterton	Lotus Cortina		Lotus	4	2nd in class		5
19/04	Sunday Mirror Trophy	Goodwood	F1 Lotus	33	Climax	V8	fastest lap	3	1
	Lavant Cup Sports Cars unlimited	Goodwood	Lotus	30	Ford Fairlane	V8	fastest lap		1
	Saloon Cars unlimited	Goodwood	Lotus Cortina		Lotus	4	fastest lap		1
25/04	Pau Grand Prix	Pau	F2 Lotus	32	Ford Cosworth	4		3	1
01/05	Tourist Trophy Heat 1	Oulton Park	Lotus	30	Ford Fairlane	V8	fastest lap	5	16
	Tourist Trophy Heat 2	Oulton Park	Lotus	30	Ford Fairlane	V8	gearbox		r
	Tourist Trophy Aggregate	Oulton Park	Lotus	30	Ford Fairlane	V8			14
31/05	Indianapolis 500	Indianapolis	USAC Lotus	38	Ford	V8		2	1
05/06	Player's 200 Heat 1	Mosport Park	Lotus	30	Ford Fairlane	V8	driveshaft		r
07/06	London Trophy Heat 1	Crystal Palace	F2 Lotus	35	Ford Cosworth	4	fastest lap	2	1
	London Trophy Heat 2	Crystal Palace	F2 Lotus	35	Ford Cosworth	4	fastest lap	1	1
	London Trophy Aggregate	Crystal Palace	F2 Lotus	35	Ford Cosworth	4			1
	Norbury Trophy	Crystal Palace	Lotus Cortina		Lotus	4	1st in class		2
13/06	BELGIAN GP	Spa-Francorchamps	F1 Lotus	33	Climax	V8	fastest lap	2	1
27/06	FRENCH GP	Clermont-Ferrand	F1 Lotus	25	Climax	V8	fastest lap	1	1
03/07	Reims Grand Prix	Reims-Gueux	F2 Lotus	35	Ford Cosworth	4			3
10/07	BRITISH GP	Silverstone	F1 Lotus	33	Climax	V8		1	1
11/07	Rouen Grand Prix	Rouen-les-Essarts	F2 Lotus	35	Ford Cosworth	4		1	1
18/07	DUTCH GP	Zandvoort	F1 Lotus	33	Climax	V8	fastest lap	2	1
01/08	GERMAN GP	Nürburgring	F1 Lotus	33	Climax	V8	fastest lap/ clinched F1 world title	1	1
08/08	Kanonloppet	Karlskoga, Sweden	F2 Lotus	32	Ford Cosworth	4	ignition		r
15/08	Mediterranean Grand Prix	Enna, Sicily	F1 Lotus	25	Climax	V8	fastest lap	1	2
22/08	Mountain climb	Ste. UrsanneLes Rangiers	USAC Lotus	38	Ford	V8	demonstration		
29/08	Swiss Mountain Grand Prix	Ollon Villars	USAC Lotus	38	Ford	V8	misfire		nc
30/08	British Eagle Trophy	Brands Hatch	F2 Lotus	35	Ford Cosworth	4	fastest lap		1
	Guards Trophy Heat 1	Brands Hatch	Lotus	40	Ford	V8			10
	Guards Trophy Heat 2	Brands Hatch	Lotus	40	Ford	V8	transmission		r
	Guards Trophy Aggregate	Brands Hatch	Lotus	40	Ford	V8			nc
	Saloon Cars unlimited	Brands Hatch	Lotus Cortina		Lotus	4	outside assistance/ fastest lap		dq
12/09	ITALIAN GP	Monza	F1 Lotus	33	Climax	V8	fastest lap/ fuel pump	1	10r
18/09	International Gold Cup	Oulton Park	F2 Lotus	35	Ford Cosworth	4	fastest lap		6
	Saloon Cars unlimited	Oulton Park	Lotus Cortina		Lotus	4	1st & fastest lap in class		2
26/09	Albi Grand Prix	Albi	F2 Lotus	35	Ford Cosworth	4			1
03/10	UNITED STATES GP	Watkins Glen	F1 Lotus	33	Climax	V8	engine	2	r
24/10	MEXICAN GP	Mexico City	F1 Lotus	33	Climax	V8	engine	1	r
31/10	Times-Mirror Grand Prix	Riverside	Lotus	40	Ford	V8			2

1966

Date	Country/event	Circuit	Car	Model	Engine	Configuration	Notes	Grid position	Result
08/01	New Zealand International GP (Tasman)	Pukekohe	F1 Lotus	39	Climax	4	gearbox	2	r
15/01	Gold Leaf International (Tasman) Heat	Levin	F1 Lotus	39	Climax	4	spin	6	r
	Gold Leaf International (Tasman) Final	Levin	F1 Lotus	39	Climax	4		3	2
	Flying Farewell	Levin	F1 Lotus	39	Climax	4			2
22/01	Lady Wigram Trophy (Tasman) Heat 1	Christchurch	F1 Lotus	39	Climax	4			2
	Lady Wigram Trophy (Tasman) Final	Christchurch	F1 Lotus	39	Climax	4	accident – hit by car with no brakes	4	r
29/01	Teretonga International (Tasman) Heat 2	Invercargill	F1 Lotus	39	Climax	4	dead heat with Jackie Stewart		1=
	Teretonga International (Tasman) Final	Invercargill	F1 Lotus	39	Climax	4	spin	1	r
13/02	Warwick Farm International (Tasman)	Warwick Farm	F1 Lotus	39	Climax	4	fastest lap	1	1
20/02	Australian Grand Prix (Tasman) Heat 2	Lakeside, Brisbane	F1 Lotus	39	Climax	4			2
20/02	Australian Grand Prix (Tasman) Final	Lakeside, Brisbane	F1 Lotus	39	Climax	4		4	3
26/02	Sandown International (Tasman) Prel	Sandown Park, Melbourne	F1 Lotus	39	Climax	4			2
27/02	Sandown International (Tasman)	Sandown Park, Melbourne	F1 Lotus	39	Climax	4		3	2
05/03	Launceston Examiner 45	Longford, Tasmania	F1 Lotus	39	Climax	4			3
07/03	South Pacific Trophy (Tasman)	Longford, Tasmania	F1 Lotus	39	Climax	4		3	7
03/04	BARC 200 'Spring Trophy'	Oulton Park	F2 Lotus	35	Ford Cosworth	4	race abandoned – snow on track	1	ns
	Saloon Cars unlimited	Oulton Park	Lotus Cortina		Lotus	4	race abandoned – snow on track	1	ns
08/04	Saloon Cars unlimited	Snetterton	Lotus Cortina		Lotus	4	1st & fastest lap in class		3
11/04	Sunday Mirror Trophy	Goodwood	F2 Lotus	35	Ford Cosworth	4	puncture		r
	Saloon Cars unlimited	Goodwood	Lotus Cortina		Lotus	4	1st & fastest lap in class		4
17/04	Pau Grand Prix	Pau	F2 Lotus	35	Ford Cosworth	4			7
24/04	Juan Jover Trophy	Montjuïc Park	F2 Lotus	44	Ford Cosworth	4	fuel pump		r
22/05	MONACO GP	Monte-Carlo	F1 Lotus	33	Climax	V8	rear suspension	1	r
30/05	Indianapolis 500	Indianapolis	USAC Lotus	38	Ford	V8		2	2
12/06	BELGIAN GP	Spa-Francorchamps	F1 Lotus	33	Climax	V8	engine	10	r
03/07	FRENCH GP	Reims-Gueux	F1 Lotus	33	Climax	V8	hit in the face by bird		ns
16/07	BRITISH GP	Brands Hatch	F1 Lotus	33	Climax	V8		5	4
24/07	DUTCH GP	Zandvoort	F1 Lotus	33	Climax	V8		3	3
07/08	GERMAN GP	Nürburgring	F1 Lotus	33	Climax	V8	accident	1	r
21/08	Kanonloppet	Karlskoga, Sweden	F2 Lotus	44	Ford Cosworth	4			3
24/08	Suomen Grand Prix Heat 1	Keimola, Finland	F2 Lotus	44	Ford Cosworth	4			3
	Suomen Grand Prix Heat 2	Keimola, Finland	F2 Lotus	44	Ford Cosworth	4			3
	Suomen Grand Prix Aggregate	Keimola, Finland	F2 Lotus	44	Ford Cosworth	4			3
29/08	Guards Trophy Heat 1	Brands Hatch	Felday	4	BRM	V8	1st & fastest lap in class	10	8
	Guards Trophy Heat 2	Brands Hatch	Felday	4	BRM	V8	black flagged – oil smoke		r
	Guards Trophy Aggregate	Brands Hatch	Felday	4	BRM	V8			nc
	Saloon Cars unlimited	Brands Hatch	Lotus Cortina		Lotus	4			1
04/09	ITALIAN GP	Monza	F1 Lotus	43	BRM	H16	gearbox	3	r
11/09	Grand Prix de l'Ile de France	Montlhéry	F2 Lotus	44	Ford Cosworth	4	fastest lap		2
17/09	International Gold Cup	Oulton Park	F1 Lotus	33	Climax	V8		5	3
	Saloon Cars unlimited	Oulton Park	Lotus Cortina		Lotus	4	class fastest lap		1
18/09	Trophée Craven 'A'	Le Mans	F2 Lotus	44	Ford Cosworth	4	throttle linkage		r
25/09	Albi Grand Prix	Albi	F2 Lotus	44	Ford Cosworth	4		2	9
02/10	UNITED STATES GP	Watkins Glen	F1 Lotus	43	BRM	H16		2	1
09/10	Indianapolis Cars	Mount Fuji, Japan	USAC Lotus	38	Ford	V8	engine		ns
23/10	MEXICAN GP	Mexico City	F1 Lotus	43	BRM	H16	gearbox	2	r
30/10	Motor Show 200 Heat 1	Brands Hatch	F2 Lotus	44	Ford Cosworth	4			3
	Motor Show 200 Final	Brands Hatch	F2 Lotus	44	Ford Cosworth	4			3
	Saloon Cars unlimited Heat 1	Brands Hatch	Lotus Cortina		Lotus	4	class fastest lap	1	1
	Saloon Cars unlimited Heat 2	Brands Hatch	Lotus Cortina		Lotus	4			15
	Saloon Cars unlimited Aggregate	Brands Hatch	Lotus Cortina		Lotus	4	3rd in class		10
1923/11	RAC Rally	Great Britain	Lotus Cortina		Lotus	4	accident		r

1967

Date	Country/event	Circuit	Car	Model	Engine	Configuration	Notes	Grid position	Result
02/01	SOUTH AFRICAN GP	Kyalami	F1 Lotus	43	BRM	H16	engine	3	r
07/01	New Zealand Grand Prix (Tasman)	Pukekohe	F1 Lotus	33	Climax	V8	fastest lap	5	2
14/01	Wills Levin International (Tasman)	Levin	F1 Lotus	33	Climax	V8	fastest lap	1	1
21/01	Lady Wigram Trophy (Tasman)	Christchurch	F1 Lotus	33	Climax	V8		3	1
28/01	Teretonga International (Tasman)	Invercargill	F1 Lotus	33	Climax	V8	fastest lap	2	1
12/02	Lakeside International (Tasman)	Lakeside, Brisbane	F1 Lotus	33	Climax	V8	fastest lap	1	1
19/02	Australian Grand Prix (Tasman)	Warwick Farm	F1 Lotus	33	Climax	V8		2	2
26/02	Sandown Park International (Tasman)	Sandown Park, Melbourne	F1 Lotus	33	Climax	V8		3	1
04/03	South Pacific Trophy Heat 1 (Tasman)	Longford, Tasmania	F1 Lotus	33	Climax	V8		4	2
	South Pacific Trophy Heat 2 (Tasman)	Longford, Tasmania	F1 Lotus	33	Climax	V8		4	3
05/03	South Pacific Trophy Final (Tasman)	Longford, Tasmania	F1 Lotus	33	Climax	V8		3	2
02/04	Pau Grand Prix	Pau	F2 Lotus	48	Ford Cosworth	4	fastest lap	1	4
09/04	Juan Jover Trophy	Montjuïc Park	F2 Lotus	48	Ford Cosworth	4	fastest lap		1
23/04	Eifelrennen	Nürburgring	F2 Lotus	48	Ford Cosworth	4	gearbox	1	r
07/05	MONACO GP	Monte-Carlo	F1 Lotus	33	Climax	V8	rear suspension/ accident/ fastest lap	5	r
21/05	Limbourg Grand Prix Heat 1	Zolder	F2 Lotus	48	Ford Cosworth	4	fastest lap	2	1
	Limbourg Grand Prix Heat 2	Zolder	F2 Lotus	48	Ford Cosworth	4		1	4
	Limbourg Grand Prix Aggregate	Zolder	F2 Lotus	48	Ford Cosworth	4			2
3031/05	Indianapolis 500	Indianapolis	USAC Lotus	38	Ford	V8	piston	16	31r
04/06	DUTCH GP	Zandvoort	F1 Lotus	49	Ford Cosworth	V8	fastest lap	8	1
18/06	BELGIAN GP	Spa-Francorchamps	F1 Lotus	49	Ford Cosworth	V8		1	6
25/06	Reims Grand Prix	Reims-Gueux	F2 Lotus	48	Ford Cosworth	4	gear selector		r
02/07	FRENCH GP	Bugatti au Mans	F1 Lotus	49	Ford Cosworth	V8	crown wheel & pinion	4	r
09/07	Rouen Grand Prix	Rouen-les-Essarts	F2 Lotus	48	Ford Cosworth	4	puncture/ accident		r
15/07	BRITISH GP	Silverstone	F1 Lotus	49	Ford Cosworth	V8		1	1
16/07	Flugplatzrennen	Tulln-Langenlebarn	F2 Lotus	48	Ford Cosworth	4	puncture/ fastest lap	3	r
23/07	Madrid Grand Prix	Jarama	F2 Lotus	48	Ford Cosworth	4	fastest lap	2	1
06/08	GERMAN GP	Nürburgring	F1 Lotus	49	Ford Cosworth	V8	front suspension	1	r
13/08	Swedish Grand Prix	Karlskoga	F2 Lotus	48	Ford Cosworth	4		3	3
20/08	Mediterranean Grand Prix Heat 1	Enna, Sicily	F2 Lotus	48	Ford Cosworth	4	engine		7r
	Mediterranean Grand Prix Heat 2	Enna, Sicily	F2 Lotus	48	Ford Cosworth	4	engine		ns
	Mediterranean Grand Prix Aggregate	Enna, Sicily	F2 Lotus	48	Ford Cosworth	4			nc
27/08	CANADIAN GP	Mosport Park	F1 Lotus	49	Ford Cosworth	V8	ignition wet	1	r
03/09	Suomen Grand Prix Preliminary Heat	Keimola, Finland	F2 Lotus	48	Ford Cosworth	4		2	1
	Suomen Grand Prix Final	Keimola, Finland	F2 Lotus	48	Ford Cosworth	4	fastest lap	1	1
05/09	Hameenlinnan Ajot	Ahvenisto, Finland	F2 Lotus	48	Ford Cosworth	4		1	3
10/09	ITALIAN GP	Monza	F1 Lotus	49	Ford Cosworth	V8	fastest lap	1	3
24/09	Albi Grand Prix	Albi	F2 Lotus	44	Ford Cosworth	4		2	3
01/10	UNITED STATES GP	Watkins Glen	F1 Lotus	49	Ford Cosworth	V8		2	1
22/10	MEXICAN GP	Mexico City	F1 Lotus	49	Ford Cosworth	V8	fastest lap	1	1
29/10	American 500 (NASCAR)	Rockingham	Ford	Fairlane	Ford	V8	engine		r
12/11	Spanish Grand Prix	Jarama	F1 Lotus	49	Ford Cosworth	V8	fastest lap	1	1
26/11	Rex Mays 300	Riverside	USAC	Vollstedt	Ford	4	engine	2	r

1968

Date	Country/event	Circuit	Car	Model	Engine	Configuration	Notes	Grid position	Result
01/01	SOUTH AFRICAN GP	Kyalami	F1 Lotus	49	Ford Cosworth	V8	final WC F1 race/ fastest lap	1	1
06/01	New Zealand Grand Prix (Tasman)	Pukekohe	F1 Lotus	49T	Ford Cosworth	V8	engine	1	r
13/01	Rothmans International (Tasman)	Levin	F1 Lotus	49T	Ford Cosworth	V8	accident damage	1	r
20/01	Lady Wigram Trophy (Tasman)	Christchurch	F1 Lotus	49T	Ford Cosworth	V8	fastest lap	1	1
27/01	Teretonga International (Tasman)	Invercargill	F1 Lotus	49T	Ford Cosworth	V8	lost nose cone/ fastest lap	2	2
11/02	Rothmans 100 (Tasman)	Surfers Paradise	F1 Lotus	49T	Ford Cosworth	V8		2	1
18/02	Warwick Farm 100 (Tasman)	Warwick Farm	F1 Lotus	49T	Ford Cosworth	V8		1	1
25/02	Australian Grand Prix (Tasman)	Sandown Park, Melbourne	F1 Lotus	49T	Ford Cosworth	V8		3	1
04/03	South Pacific Trophy (Tasman)	Longford, Tasmania	F1 Lotus	49T	Ford Cosworth	V8		1	5
31/03	Barcelona Grand Prix 'Juan Jover Trophy'	Montjuïc Park	F2 Lotus	48	Ford Cosworth	4	accident	2	r
07/04	Deutschland Trophy Heat 1	Hockenheim	F2 Lotus	48	Ford Cosworth	4	fatal accident	7	